Keys to Homeownership
2nd Edition

Founded in 1951, the National Foundation for Credit Counseling, Inc.® (NFCC), through its member agencies, sets the national standard for quality credit counseling, debt reduction services, and financial literacy training. As the nation's largest and longest serving nonprofit credit counseling organization, NFCC has played the key role in providing financial counseling and education to consumers for more than 50 years. With 115 member agencies and nearly 1,000 local offices throughout the country, the NFCC is the national voice for its members, which are nonprofit, mission driven, community-based agencies.

Worksheets 67

Preface

You want to buy a house—a place of your own. You're probably excited and a bit nervous at the prospect, especially if you're a first-time home-buyer. Our goal in publishing this guide is to take the confusion and uncertainty out of the home-buying process. Whatever your concerns about buying a home, this guide should help you feel more confident as you undertake what will probably be the largest purchase of your lifetime. In fact, by the time you complete this guide, you will probably know more about the home-buying process, and the financial planning that goes with it, than many current homeowners.

This guide will take you through the home-buying process step by step—from deciding whether homeownership is right for you to shopping for a house that meets your needs, obtaining a home mortgage, closing the sale, maintaining the house after it's yours, and successfully handling your mortgage obligation.

Chapter 1 begins by helping you determine whether you're prepared financially for homeownership. It answers questions such as these: Can I afford to buy a house and, if so, how expensive a house? How much cash will I need? How much money will I be able to borrow? Will I be able to get a mortgage if I have had past credit problems? What if I don't have an established credit history? What types of mortgages are available, and how should I decide which one is best for me? If I'm not able to buy right now, what can I do so that

I'll be better prepared to buy a house in another year or two?

Chapter 2 guides you through the process of deciding what features in a home are important to you, and then shopping for a home that is afford-able and meets your needs. It answers questions such as these: Does it have to cost me anything to have a real estate sales professional show me houses? When I'm shown a house, what should I be looking for? If I'm interested in a house, should I sign a "purchase and sale agreement" so another buyer won't get it first? Do I need to hire a real estate attorney for guidance? When I find a house I want to buy, can I offer the seller less than the asking price? What if I discover a problem with the house after I've already agreed to buy it?

Chapter 3 explains the ins and outs of shopping for a mortgage. It answers questions such as these: Do all financial institutions offer pretty much the same interest rates? How can I shop for a lender that offers the most attractive terms on the type of mortgage I want? How will the lender decide whether to give me a loan? If my loan application is rejected, what are my options?

Chapter 4 concentrates on the closing or settle-ment—the day when your loan becomes final, your mortgage is issued, and you finally receive the keys to your new home. We answer questions such as these: Should my lawyer come to the closing? What papers will I be expected to sign? Why does it cost thousands of dollars just to get a loan? What fees will I be charged?

Chapter 5 takes a closer look at the responsibilities that come with homeownership (maintaining the house and making your monthly mortgage payments) and the possible financial benefits (taking tax deductions and building equity in your home). Once again we try to anticipate questions you may have, such as these: What are the tax advantages of homeownership? If I get behind in my mortgage payments, could I really lose my home? How can I save for emergencies when I can barely make ends meet? When is refinancing my mortgage loan a good idea?

At the back of the guide is a **Glossary**. By becoming familiar with these terms before you begin house hunting, you won't be uncertain when you hear them being used by real estate professionals, loan officers, or settlement agents.

Acknowledgments

The National Foundation for Credit Counseling, Inc. (NFCC) is grateful to Fannie Mae for making this publication possible. "Keys to Homeownership" is the successor publication to Fannie Mae's "Guide to Homeownership." We owe a great debt of gratitude to Fannie Mae and its external review team for the development of the original guide.

In addition, the NFCC wishes to thank the following people for their valuable feedback in updating this publication.

Jody Anderson, Lutheran Social Services
Hubie Ashcraft, CCCS of Northeast Indiana
Bettye Banks, CCCS of Greater Dallas
Jan Britt, CCCS of Greater New Orleans
Linda Cade, CCCS of Southern Oregon
Rich Call, CCCS of the Midwest
Sandra Dunaway, CCCS of Mobile

Karen Hiller, HCCI
Natalie Kaibel, CCCS of Midwest
Margo Mitchell, CCCS of Oklahoma
Virginia Peschke, CCCS of McHenry County
Peggy Sarbaugh-McNally, CCCS of McHenry County
Bill Thompson, CCCS of Jacksonville

CHAPTER 1

Preparing for Homeownership

Overview

For many Americans, owning their own home is the American dream. If homeownership is your dream, too, it can become a reality, but not without realistic goals, sound advice, careful planning, and a clear understanding of the costs involved. As in any new endeavor, the more you know about homeownership, the better you will be able to reach your goals. This opening chapter will help you decide if homeownership is right for you and whether you can afford to buy a home at the present time. It also will provide you with a good idea of how much home you can get for your money and what mortgage lenders look for in approving a loan. Finally, it will show how first-time homebuyers and low- and moderate-income households can stretch their borrowing power with a variety of flexible mortgage products—products that can help you make your dream of homeownership come true.

Approved by the U.S. Department of Housing and Urban Development (HUD), the National Foundation for Credit Counseling, Inc. (NFCC) is a national intermediary for local housing counseling agencies. The first step on your journey to homeownership should begin with a counseling session with a HUD-approved agency. For immediate referral to a HUD-approved, NFCC member agency, please call our housing counseling referral line at (866) 845-2227.

Do you really want to own your own home?

Have you considered what it is about owning your own home that you find appealing? The decision to buy a home is certainly not one to be made lightly because owning a home requires a significant investment in time, energy, and money. Therefore, the best way to start the home-buying process is by taking a realistic look at what you can expect from homeownership and what owning your own home implies. There are many good reasons for buying a home, provided you're ready for the increased responsibilities that come with homeownership.

Advantages of Homeownership

If you are planning to buy a home, you probably have good reasons in mind, ranging from the purely personal to the very practical.

A place of your own...
Your home can be your castle and a place to call your own. Perhaps you are ready to settle down in your community, and want the feeling of permanence and involvement that comes with owning your own home. Perhaps you need more space to raise a family. Or, maybe you want more flexibility than you have in a rental unit to adapt your living space to suit your individual taste and needs.

Financial incentives...

For many people, the motivation for homeownership is primarily financial. Owning your own home can be a sound financial investment as well as a way to reduce your tax obligations.

Scheduled savings...

When you buy a house, your monthly mortgage payments serve as a type of scheduled savings plan. Over time you gradually accumulate what lenders call "equity," an ownership interest in the property that you can often borrow against or convert into cash by selling the house. In contrast, renters must continue paying rent to a landlord for as long as they rent, without the opportunity to build up equity.

Stable housing costs. Another advantage of homeownership is that while rents typically increase year after year, the principal and interest portions of "fixed-rate" mortgage payments remain unchanged throughout the entire repayment period, which is 30 years for a 30-year fixed-rate mortgage. In fact, because of the effect of inflation, this means that over the years you pay the same amount but with ever "cheaper" dollars. However, taxes and insurance are also part of the borrower's monthly payment and they can fluctuate. They are generally held in an escrow account for the payment of the borrower's state and local property taxes as well as insurance premiums.

Note: with an adjustable-rate mortgage or ARM, the interest portion of the mortgage payments may increase if interest rates increase. See the "Alternative financing mortgages" section below for further detail.

Increased value. Houses may increase in value, or appreciate, over time. In certain parts of the country, it's not unusual to find that a house that sold for $100,000 15 years ago is worth a much higher amount today. This increased worth (equity) is as good as money in the bank to the homeowner.

Tax benefits. Homeowners also get significant tax breaks not available to renters. Most importantly, interest paid on a home mortgage is usually deductible. This alone can save you a substantial amount each year in federal and state income taxes. The tax benefits of homeownership are discussed in more detail in Chapter 5.

Possible Drawbacks to Homeownership

Despite its many attractions, homeownership is not for everybody. For one thing, buying a home is a complex, time-consuming, and costly process that brings with it sometimes unwelcomed responsibility.

High cost of homeownership...

Buying a house can put considerable strain on a family's finances. Even if your mortgage payments are less than you paid previously in rent, you must also pay property taxes, homeowner's insurance, utilities, and upkeep expenses.

Possibility of foreclosure...

Foreclosure is the sale of a mortgaged property (your home) by the lender when the borrower fails to make monthly mortgage payments on a timely basis or otherwise defaults on the mortgage. A mortgage represents a large financial obligation extending over a long period of time.

Financial institutions can foreclose when borrowers fail to keep up with their payments. This can result not only in the loss of your home but also in the loss of your investment and good credit rating.

Decreased mobility...

Homeowners also have less mobility than renters. A homebuyer cannot move after simply giving the required notice to the landlord. If you anticipate being transferred to a new job location within the next year or two, this might not be the ideal time to buy a house.

Repairs and maintenance...

Many people shy away from buying a house because they don't want the responsibility of maintenance (mowing the lawn, taking care of needed repairs, etc.). Condominiums are popular for this reason—homeownership without the repair and maintenance responsibilities.

Can you afford to buy a house?

If you're convinced that you want to buy a house, you need to consider whether you can afford it. You don't want to find yourself without a penny to spare for anything else. And you don't want to overextend yourself to the point where you can't keep up with your mortgage payments and risk losing the house.

Analyzing Your Current Expenses

Many new homeowners find that when they add up their total housing costs (the monthly mortgage payment; the cost of moving, settling in, and making immediate repairs; and the ongoing costs of taxes, insurance, and property maintenance), these costs are higher than the amount they previously paid for rent. If you think this might be true for you, can you afford to pay more for housing? Do you usually have some money left at the end of each pay period? If not, you may need to change some of your spending habits before you can consider buying a house.

If you have never planned a budget, you may not have a clear idea of how you spend your money. If this is your situation, you need to take a look at your spending patterns. To get started, turn to Chapter 5 for guidance on developing a budget.

Notice that some of your expenses are fixed, such as your car payment, taxes, and day care; others are discretionary—that is, you have considerable flexibility in deciding how much or how little to spend in these areas (for example, clothing and entertainment).

To some extent, you must simply decide how important it is to own your own home. Are you willing to put off some purchases or spend less for a time? You can try out the cost of homeownership by putting aside extra funds each month or from each paycheck. If you find you can do this, you may indeed be ready for homeownership.

You should not consider buying a house until you can handle the mortgage payment and other housing-related costs. If you do not repay your mortgage as promised in the mortgage documents you sign, you may lose your home!

The Costs of Purchasing a Home

Let's look at the main costs involved in purchasing a home. These include the upfront costs and the ongoing costs.

Up-front costs...

Your up-front costs will include the down payment, closing (or settlement) costs, and the expense of moving and settling into your new home. It can also include "earnest money" or a deposit that the homebuyer puts down on the home to impress the seller that the buyer "earnestly" intends to purchase the home.

Down payment. Virtually all homebuyers rely on a loan (or mortgage) from a financial institution. And most mortgage products require that you contribute some portion of your own funds (the down payment). Lenders feel more secure if you have money invested in the house; that way you are not likely to walk away from it if your finances take a turn for the worse.

In the past, lenders expected buyers to make a down payment of at least 20 percent of the purchase price. This meant that buyers needed a down payment of $30,000 to buy a $150,000 house. Today, buyers can pay as little as zero to 5 percent down provided they purchase private mortgage insurance (or PMI), which helps protect the lender in case the borrower fails to repay the loan. A 5 percent down payment on that $150,000 home comes to $7,500. However, PMI might add another $100 to the monthly payment.

Closing costs. Besides the down payment, homebuyers must be prepared to pay a number of additional up-front costs incurred in buying a home. Collectively called "closing costs" (discussed in Chapter 4), these expenses range from 3 percent to

6 percent of the mortgage. (In some areas of the country, closing costs may be even higher than 6 percent.)

If you were to buy a $150,000 house with a 5 percent down payment ($7,500), you could expect to pay $4,275 to $8,550 in closing costs on your $142,500 mortgage. (Your local NFCC housing counseling agency can help you find down payment assistance programs for first-time and low-income buyers.)

Settling-in costs. You also will need to consider what it will cost to move and settle into a new home. If you buy a house needing immediate repairs, you will need money after buying the house. You also may need to purchase major appliances such as a stove and refrigerator. You do not want to spend all of your money on buying the house.

Ongoing costs...

As a renter, your primary housing cost is the amount of your monthly rent payment. As a homeowner, your housing costs will include your monthly mortgage payment, property taxes, homeowner's insurance, mortgage insurance (if required by the lender), utilities, and maintenance. Owners of condominiums or cooperatives also pay a monthly maintenance fee, often called a "homeowners' association fee" or "carrying charge."

Monthly mortgage payment. Since most homebuyers are accustomed to paying rent monthly, they are usually prepared to make monthly mortgage payments. Each mortgage payment includes both the repayment of a portion of the principal (the amount you actually borrowed) and the interest (a fee for using the lender's funds). Lenders refer to payments of principal and interest as "P&I."

The amount of your monthly payment depends on the amount you borrow, the interest rate, the repayment period (or term), and whether you have a fixed- or adjustable-rate mortgage. For example:

Size of mortgage	Interest rate	Term	Monthly Payments (P&I only)
$100,000	8%	30 years	$734
$100,000	8%	15 years	$956

Chart 1, "Calculate your payment," shows how the loan amount and the interest rate affect the monthly payment. As the chart indicates, the bigger the loan amount and the higher the interest rate, the larger the borrower's monthly payment. You may wonder how these monthly payments are calculated. Most mortgages are fully "amortized." This means that at the end of the repayment period (after 30 years of making the same monthly principal and interest payment), you will have paid the entire amount of principal and all the interest charged by the lender. The house is then yours, free and clear.

Taxes and insurance (T&I). In many cases, a homebuyer's monthly mortgage payments include not only the amount required to repay a portion of the principal and accrued interest (P&I) but also property taxes, homeowner's insurance, and private mortgage insurance. The lender holds these additional amounts in a separate "escrow" account and then pays the tax and insurance bills. In this way, the lender ensures that these annual expenses get paid on time. If taxes and insurance are not escrowed each month, the homeowner must be prepared to pay these bills when they are due.

Because taxes and insurance are an essential part of a homeowner's housing costs, lenders often refer to the components of a mortgage payment as PITI, or principal, interest, taxes, and insurance. Condominium and cooperative fees belong in this category as well.

Other costs. Other ongoing costs include utilities (oil, gas, electricity, and water) and maintenance costs. First-time homebuyers often are surprised by the high cost of basic upkeep. The cost of utilities

Chart 1. Calculate your Mortgage Payment

The amount of your monthly mortgage payment will depend on how much you borrow, the term (repayment period) of the loan, and the interest rate. If you know how much you need to borrow (the purchase price minus your down payment) and what the interest rate will be, you can use this chart to find what your monthly principal and interest payment will be if you get a standard 30-year fixed-rate mortgage. Note that this chart includes only principal and interest payments, not property taxes, hazard insurance, and private mortgage insurance.

Loan Amount ($)	Interest Rate												
	6%	6.5%	7%	7.5%	8%	8.5%	9%	9.5%	10%	10.5%	11%	11.5%	12%
40,000	240	253	266	280	294	308	322	336	351	366	381	396	411
45,000	270	284	299	315	330	346	362	378	395	412	429	446	463
50,000	300	316	333	350	367	384	402	420	439	457	476	495	514
55,000	330	348	366	385	404	423	443	462	483	503	524	545	566
60,000	360	379	399	420	440	461	483	505	527	549	571	594	617
65,000	390	411	432	454	477	500	523	547	570	595	619	644	669
70,000	420	442	466	489	514	538	563	589	614	640	667	693	720
75,000	450	474	499	524	550	577	603	631	658	686	714	743	771
80,000	480	506	532	559	587	615	644	673	702	732	762	792	823
85,000	510	537	566	594	624	654	684	715	746	778	810	842	874
90,000	540	569	599	629	660	692	724	757	790	823	857	891	926
95,000	570	600	632	664	697	731	764	799	834	869	905	941	977
100,000	600	632	665	699	734	769	805	841	878	915	952	990	1029
110,000	660	695	732	769	807	846	885	925	965	1006	1048	1089	1131
120,000	720	758	798	839	881	923	966	1009	1053	1098	1143	1188	1234
130,000	780	822	865	909	954	1000	1046	1093	1141	1189	1238	1287	1337
140,000	840	885	932	979	1027	1077	1126	1177	1229	1281	1333	1386	1440
150,000	900	948	998	1049	1101	1153	1207	1261	1316	1372	1429	1485	1543
160,000	960	1011	1065	1119	1174	1230	1287	1345	1404	1464	1524	1584	1646
170,000	1020	1074	1131	1189	1247	1307	1368	1429	1492	1555	1619	1683	1749
180,000	1080	1138	1198	1259	1321	1384	1448	1513	1580	1647	1714	1782	1851
190,000	1140	1201	1264	1328	1394	1461	1529	1598	1667	1738	1810	1881	1954
200,000	1200	1264	1331	1398	1468	1538	1609	1682	1755	1830	1905	1980	2057
210,000	1260	1327	1397	1468	1541	1615	1690	1766	1843	1921	2000	2079	2160
220,000	1320	1390	1464	1538	1614	1692	1770	1850	1931	2013	2095	2178	2263
230,000	1380	1454	1530	1608	1688	1769	1851	1934	2018	2104	2190	2278	2366

may vary greatly (increasing during the heating season, for example), but repairs often are an unexpected expense. For these reasons, homeowners always must have a cash reserve.

But the news is not all bad: Homeowners receive significant federal income tax benefits (see Chapter 5).

We've looked at both your budget and the expenses of homeownership. Before you begin house hunting, you need to know what you can afford.

How much home can you afford?

An often-quoted rule says you can afford a house that costs up to two and one-half times your annual gross income (that is, the amount you make before taxes are deducted). If you are buying a house with someone else (spouse, parent, adult child, partner/companion, brother or sister, etc.) you can consider your co-purchaser's annual gross income in deciding how expensive a home you can buy. (Your co-purchaser's debts and credit history also will determine how much you can borrow. The co-purchaser also is liable for repayment of the mortgage.) According to this guideline, if you and your co-purchaser together have an annual income totaling $80,000, you should expect to buy a home priced at no more than $200,000; if you have a joint income of $40,000, your new home should cost no more than $100,000.

This provides a ballpark figure of what you can pay for a home. If you have access to the Internet, Web-based mortgage calculators can give you a more complete picture. (See Internet resources later in this chapter.)

Your buying power ultimately depends on three things:

- How much you have available for the down payment;
- How much a financial institution will agree to lend you; and
- Your credit situation.

Let's look first at what resources you may be able to tap for your down payment and closing costs. Then we will look at the guidelines lenders use to determine how much they will loan a homebuyer. Finally, we'll discuss credit.

Your Down Payment

If you are a first-time homebuyer, the price you can afford to pay for a house may be limited by the required down payment and closing costs. Unlike homeowners who can rely on their equity in a property they already own, your savings are probably your principal resource. If you haven't accumulated much savings, you may need to set aside funds for a down payment on a regular basis from your paycheck.

Worksheet 2 (page 69), "Your available cash and assets," provides funding sources for your down payment and closing costs.

The size of your down payment determines how large a mortgage you need.

$ 200,000	purchase price	
−10,000	5 percent down payment	
$ 190,000	mortgage amount	

$ 100,000	purchase price	
−5,000	5 percent down payment	
$ 95,000	mortgage amount	

Your Borrowing Power

Apart from your down payment, the other major factor limiting how expensive a home you can buy will be how much you can borrow. When you apply for a mortgage, the lender will primarily consider three factors in determining how large a loan to grant you:

- Earnings;
- Existing debt level; and
- Credit (payment) history.

Chart 2. How Large a Mortgage Do You Qualify For?

You can use this chart to find out how large a mortgage you can qualify for based on your annual income and interest rates currently being quoted for 30 year mortgages. This chart uses Fannie Mae's "Community Homebuyer Program" as an example, so other loan programs will provide different results.

Interest Rate	Annual Income										
	$20,000	$25,000	$30,000	$35,000	$40,000	$45,000	$50,000	$55,000	$60,000	$65,000	$70,000
6.5%	$62,975	$78,720	$94,460	$110,210	$125,950	$141,695	$157,440	$173,186	$188,930	$204,675	$220,415
7%	$60,665	$75,830	$91,000	$106,170	$121,336	$136,500	$151,665	$166,835	$182,005	$197,170	$212,335
7.5%	$58,480	$73,100	$87,720	$102,340	$116,960	$131,580	$146,200	$160,820	$175,440	$190,060	$204,860
8%	$56,405	$70,510	$84,610	$98,715	$112,815	$126,915	$141,020	$155,120	$169,225	$183,325	$197,425
8.5%	$54,445	$68,055	$81,664	$95,280	$108,890	$122,500	$136,110	$149,725	$163,335	$176,945	$190,560
9%	$52,585	$65,730	$78,880	$92,025	$105,170	$118,320	$131,465	$144,610	$157,760	$170,905	$184,050
9.5%	$50,825	$63,530	$76,235	$88,945	$101,650	$114,355	$127,060	$139,770	$152,475	$165,180	$177,890
10%	$49,155	$61,445	$73,735	$86,025	$98,315	$110,605	$122,895	$135,185	$147,470	$159,760	$172,060
10.5%	$47,575	$59,740	$71,365	$83,260	$95,150	$107,045	$118,940	$130,836	$142,730	$154,625	$166,520
11%	$46,080	$57,600	$69,120	$80,635	$92,115	$103,675	$115,195	$126,715	$138,235	$149,755	$161,275

* Data provided by Fannie Mae, uses 33% of gross income as the qualifying ratio, but does not consider existing debt, which could reduce the amount for which you could qualify.

Lenders' qualifying guidelines...
Lenders use two qualifying guidelines to determine the size mortgage for which you are eligible.

- Your monthly costs (including mortgage payments, property taxes, insurance, and condominium or cooperative fee, if applicable) should total no more than 28 percent of your monthly gross (before-tax) income.
- Your monthly housing costs plus other long-term debts should total no more than 36 percent of your monthly gross income.

Lenders and financial advisors recommend that you spend no more than 25-28 percent of your income on housing and not more than 33-36 percent on total debt (housing, credit cards, and other debts). In certain situations, you can exceed these amounts, but they are a good start for a first-time homebuyer. Some local, state, and federal programs have limits on the percentage of debt someone can have in order to participate. Please talk to your NFCC HUD-approved local housing counseling agency for more information.

There are many excellent online resources to help you determine the right-sized mortgage for you. The following are several examples:

Bank Rate
www.bankrate.com/brm/mortgage-calculator.asp

Fannie Mae
www.mortgagecontent.net/scApplication/fanniemae/affordability.do

Freddie Mac
www.freddiemac.com/corporate/buyown/
english/calcs_tools

When you apply for a mortgage, the lender will use all the relevant data—your income, your existing debts, the purchase price of the house, your down payment, the interest rate on the loan, and the cost of property taxes and insurance—and quickly calculate whether you qualify for the amount you need to buy the house.

Note that qualifying for a loan is only the first step in being approved. The qualification process determines how large a mortgage you are eligible for if your loan application is approved. We discuss the loan application process in more detail in Chapter 3, including what factors lenders consider in approving or disapproving a mortgage.

Pre-qualifying yourself…

A smart move for first-time homebuyers is to get "pre-qualified" by your lender. This determines the price range in which you should shop and if there are credit issues to address prior to a home purchase.

Your gross income. In calculating your gross (before-tax) income, you can count all income that you get on a regular basis, from whatever source. Worksheet 3 (page 71), "Your gross monthly income," lists sources of income that you should consider.

Your debt payments. Lenders will also consider your existing debt in determining how large a mortgage to grant you. They are interested in your "long-term debt," any debt that will take more than 10 months to pay off. Use Worksheet 4 (page 73), "Your monthly debt payments," to tally your debts.

If your monthly debt payments are excessive for your income level (based on the qualifying guidelines), this will reduce the amount you can borrow to buy a house. Use Chart 3, "How Much Debt it Too Much?" to see where you stand. For every $50 of "excess debt," you can expect about a $5,000

reduction in the amount of mortgage you qualify for. If your debts are excessive, consider paying off some of your debt in preparation for buying a house. You will qualify for a larger mortgage, which may mean you can afford more house with your income.

Your Credit Record

As part of the "prequalification" process or as you begin the homebuying adventure, obtain a copy of your credit report. Knowing what's on your credit report can help the loan application process go smoothly. The lender also will pull a credit report as part of the application process, but it's wise to get your own copy each year.

You can obtain a free copy of your credit report from www.annualcreditreport.com, or for a small fee, you can request your credit profile from a credit reporting agency (look in the Yellow Pages or see our Internet resources section at the end of this chapter.). NFCC recommends that you obtain what's known as a "tri-merge" credit score, which is a combination of all three credit reporting bureaus.

Credit scoring…

Credit scoring is a statistical method used to predict the likelihood that a potential borrower will repay a credit obligation, such as a mortgage loan.

A credit score is based ONLY on information in a credit report:

- Previous credit performance;
- Current level of indebtedness;
- Amount of time credit has been in use;
- Pursuit of new credit; and
- Types of credit available.

A credit score is NOT based on factors prohibited under the Equal Credit Opportunity Act (ECOA), such as race, gender, color, religion, national origin, and marital status. Excluded from the credit score formula are income, employment, and residence.

Chart 3. How Much Debt is Too Much?

Use this chart to find out how much monthly debt most lenders find acceptable for borrowers at your income level. Then compare this figure with your actual monthly debt (see Worksheet 4, page 73). If your actual debt exceeds the allowable debt, this will reduce the amount of mortgage you qualify for.

Gross Annual Income	Allowable Debt Payments
$20,000	$133
25,000	167
30,000	200
35,000	233
40,000	267
45,000	300
50,000	333
55,000	367
60,000	400
65,000	432
70,000	467
75,000	500
80,000	534

The FICO score, developed by the Fair Isaac Corporation, is the most common credit score used in mortgage lending. The broad categories of credit data that are included in a FICO credit score are:

- **Payment history (approximately 35 percent of your FICO score).** Have you been late paying bills? If so, how recently did these late payments occur? How long did you remain delinquent on any bill at one time? What is the highest level of delinquency reached in the last year? How many months have passed since the most recent negative item on record (a judgment, lien, bankruptcy, etc.)? (Generally, the "worse" your credit performance is, the "worse" your credit score. Recent bad credit has a more negative impact.)

- **Amounts owed (approximately 30 percent of your FICO score).** How many consumer loans and open charge accounts do you have? What is the ratio of revolving debt to total revolving limits available to you? What is the percentage outstanding on open installment loans? (Generally, the higher the percentage of utilization of credit, the higher the risk. So DO NOT max out your credit cards!)

- **Length of credit history (approximately 15 percent of your FICO score).** How long have you had credit? (Generally, the longer you have had credit and have successfully managed your debts, the better the credit score. However, even if you have a relatively new credit history or only one or two traditional accounts, you can obtain high scores as well.)

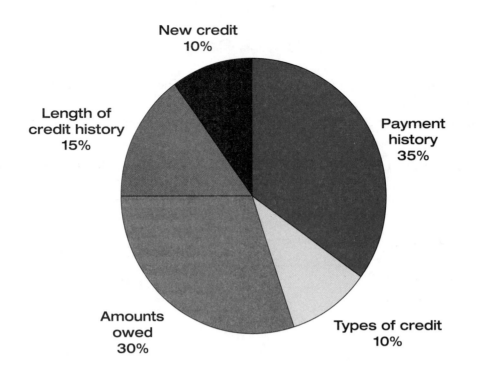

New credit segment — pie chart:

- New credit 10%
- Length of credit history 15%
- Payment history 35%
- Amounts owed 30%
- Types of credit 10%

- **New credit (approximately 10 percent of your FICO score).** Are you pursuing new sources of credit, such as an automobile loan? To measure such activity accurately, the credit score calculation only takes inquiries you initiated into account.

The score takes into account inquiries over a 12-month period. Any inquiries related to automobiles and mortgages that occurred over the past 30 days are excluded. And if multiple automobile or mortgage-related inquiries occur in any 14-day period, they are considered a single inquiry.

The credit score model does not include inquiries you did not initiate. For example, banks mail promotions to consumers to whom they would LIKE to issue a credit card. Such inquiries appear on your report as PRM or promotional inquiries and do not influence your credit score.

- **Types of credit in use (approximately 10 percent of your FICO score).** What types of credit do you have? Department store credit cards? Bank-issued credit cards? Installment

credit with a local furniture store? (Generally, the types of credit available are not as important a factor in determining a credit score as the other categories.)

Establishing a credit record...
If you have no credit record either good or bad, now is the time to establish one. If you do not have a traditional credit record that shows payments made on credit card purchases, a car loan, or student loan, it is still possible to establish a credit history. For example, you can build a nontraditional credit history by documenting your monthly rent payments to previous landlords; utility companies for electricity, gas, water, and telephone services; cable television companies; or insurance companies for medical, automobile, and life insurance.

Repairing a bad credit record...
You also may find that your credit record is not as clean as you might wish. If you are currently having credit problems, you may not be able to buy a house until they are resolved. If your problems are in the past, your recent track record of timely debt

payment may help. By law, most unfavorable credit information must be dropped from your credit file after seven years. A bankruptcy remains on your credit report for 10 years.

If you are behind on your bills and feel overwhelmed by debt, consider credit counseling. NFCC member agencies have nearly 1,000 offices around the country and can help develop a plan for improving your credit profile. To contact a credit counselor, call (800) 388-2227 or visit our Web site at www.nfcc.org.

Dealing with incorrect information on your credit record...
Unfortunately, credit reports sometimes are inaccurate or give a misleading picture of past credit problems that have since been resolved.

To avoid any unpleasant surprises, you should obtain a copy of your credit report right now. You don't want to take the chance of being denied a mortgage because of an erroneous credit report. If you find errors, you should correct your report before applying for a mortgage. If you have an unresolved dispute with a creditor, the credit agency must include your explanation of the situation in future credit reports. Make it a habit to check your credit report every year, moving forward.

How can you increase your borrowing power?

What if, having gone through the prequalification process, you are dissatisfied with the mortgage amount you will qualify for? Perhaps you can see that your house-buying options will be fairly limited. You may need to lower your sights and simply recognize that you'll have to buy a less expensive starter home. But before you reach that conclusion, consider ways to increase your borrowing power:

- Reduce your existing long-term debt;
- Wait to apply for a mortgage until your income increases; and/or
- Find a financing option that results in a lower down payment and lower monthly mortgage payments.

We have already seen that if your existing debt is too high in relation to your income, you can qualify for a larger mortgage by paying off some of this debt before you apply for a mortgage. When you are anticipating buying a home, it is not the time to purchase an expensive item, like a car. If it is your income limiting your borrowing capacity, you may need to try a different approach. You may wait to apply for a mortgage until your income increases or your expenses decrease. Alternatively, you can consider different financing options, some of which are outlined in the following chapters. If you have questions not answered in this book, call an NFCC housing counselor at (866) 845-2227.

Mortgage Insurance

Unless you have sufficient funds to make a 20 percent down payment, your loan will almost always require mortgage insurance. Mortgage insurance helps protect the lender if the buyer fails to repay a loan. Loans that are insured by the government or a private mortgage insurer enable the homebuyer to purchase a home with a lower down payment than would otherwise be acceptable to the lender. Mortgage insurance on government loans is known as Mortgage Insurance Premium (MIP); the term Private Mortgage Insurance (PMI) is used for all other loans.

We have already mentioned that with PMI, lenders will reduce the down payment requirement from 20 percent of the purchase price to as low as 3 percent. On a $100,000 home, instead of putting down $20,000, you might be able to make a down payment as low as $3,000! The PMI cost will be added to your monthly mortgage payments and your closing costs.

Government-insured loans...
Mortgage insurance also is available through three federal government programs: the Federal Housing Administration (FHA) mortgage insurance program operated by the U.S. Department of Housing and Urban Development (HUD), the Department of Veterans Affairs' (VA) loan guarantee program, and the Rural Housing Service

(RHS) loan program. To obtain any of these loans, you apply through a lender approved to handle them.

FHA loans. With FHA insurance, you can purchase a home with a very low down payment (from 3 percent to 5 percent of the FHA appraisal value or the purchase price, whichever is lower). FHA mortgages have a maximum loan limit that varies depending on the average cost of housing in a given region. For more information, visit www.hud.gov/buying/loans.cfm.

VA loans. The VA guarantee allows qualified veterans to buy homes with low or no down payment and with less strict guidelines than FHA or conventional loans. If you are a qualified veteran, this can be an attractive mortgage program. To determine whether you are eligible, check with your nearest VA regional office. For more information, visit www.homeloans.va.gov/veteran.htm.

Rural Housing Service (RHS) loans. The Rural Housing Service, formerly known as the Farmers Home Administration and a branch of the U.S. Department of Agriculture, offers low interest rate homeownership loans with no down payments to low- and moderate-income persons living in rural areas. Check with your local RHS office or a local lender for eligibility requirements. For more information, visit www.rurdev.usda.gov/rhs/common/indiv_intro.htm.

Teacher/Officer Next Door Programs. HUD operates teachers and law enforcement officers housing programs where these community servants can purchase HUD housing at a reduced cost. There are strict residency requirements for this program. More information is available at the links below or by contacting your local NFCC housing counseling agency.

Teachers:
www.hud.gov/offices/hsg/sfh/reo/goodn/tnd.cfm

Officers:
www.hud.gov/offices/hsg/sfh/reo/goodn/ond.cfm

State and local loan programs. A number of states sponsor programs to help first-time homebuyers qualify for mortgages. Local housing agencies also offer attractive loan terms to eligible homebuyers in some areas. These loan terms often include low down payments or low interest rates to first-time homebuyers that meet specified income guidelines. Check with your state or local housing agency. The phone numbers usually can be found in the government "blue pages" of the phone book.

Other Types of Mortgages

Many lenders offer a wide variety of mortgage types, some specifically geared toward helping first-time homebuyers qualify for a larger loan.

Adjustable-rate mortgage (ARM)...
With a fixed-rate mortgage, the homeowner's monthly principal and interest payments never change because the interest rate is fixed for the life of the loan. With an adjustable-rate mortgage (ARM), the interest rate paid by the borrower is adjusted from time to time to bring it in line with changing market rates. This means that when interest rates go up, your monthly mortgage payments go up as well, sometimes significantly. On the other hand, when interest rates go down, your monthly mortgage payment also should go down.

ARMs are attractive to some borrowers because they initially may offer a lower interest rate than fixed-rate mortgages. Since the monthly payments on an ARM start out lower than for a fixed-rate mortgage of the same amount, the homebuyer qualifies for a larger loan. The chief drawback is that your monthly payments will increase when interest rates go up. How much your payments can increase will depend on the terms of your mortgage. Before agreeing to an ARM, be sure you know how high your monthly payments could possibly go—the so-called worst case scenario. (Most mortgage lending institutions are required by law to provide you with this worst-case scenario.)

You may want to consider an ARM if it's the only way you can afford a home and you're confident that your income will increase in the coming years. The various protective features you should look for when you shop for an ARM are discussed in Chapter 3. If you're not confident that your income will increase, you should consider buying a house that you can afford now.

Seller take-back mortgage...

If you assume an existing low-interest mortgage, the balance on the mortgage will usually be far less than the purchase price of the house. This means you must come up with a large down payment unless you can get the owner to finance part of the difference. Sometimes sellers are willing to take back a second mortgage, sometimes at a below-market interest rate. Just be sure you can afford both mortgages.

Fannie Mae and Freddie Mac Community Lending...

Fannie Mae and Freddie Mac offer low- and moderate-income households financing options that are designed to overcome the most common barriers to homeownership. For households of modest means, these barriers include down payment and closing costs and managing housing expenses that often are higher than the qualifying guidelines permitted.

They also allow borrowers to use a nontraditional credit history. For example, if you do not have a credit history, your history of timely payment to utility companies, current and previous landlords, and other sources of credit or service may be used.

These options are offered in partnership with lenders, mortgage insurers, government agencies, and nonprofit organizations across the country. To be eligible for many of these programs, your income must be no more than the median area income.

These agencies frequently require homebuyer education classes, which provide former renters with the tools and skills needed to take on the responsibilities of homeownership. You may be required to participate in homebuyer education to be eligible for the loan, but even if you are not, we strongly recommend you attend a class. Homebuyer education classes are usually available in most areas through a HUD-approved housing counseling agency.

Subsidized second mortgage loans...

Many lenders also have subsidized (financially assisted) second mortgages. The funds for subsidized second mortgages are provided by federal, city, county, and state housing agencies, as well as foundations and nonprofit organizations.

The typical financing for this mortgage product includes a down payment from your own funds, a first mortgage for most of the financing, and a subsidized second mortgage that may cover part of the down payment and/or closing costs. (This allows the limited public or nonprofit funds that are earmarked for homeownership subsidies to be used to help the greatest number of homebuyers possible.) You must provide a minimum down payment, usually 3 percent to 5 percent of the purchase price.

Subsidized second mortgages offer several features that can help close the affordability gap on a home purchase. Their payment is often deferred (delayed), they carry no or very low interest rates, and part of the debt may be forgiven for each year that you remain in the home. Also, you may use part of the subsidy to pay for closing or rehabilitation costs not covered in the sales price.

Rehabilitation Loans

Lenders with strong rehabilitation lending experience may offer Community Home Improvement Mortgage Loans. With this type of loan, you can usually obtain 95 percent financing for the purchase and improvement of a home in need of modest repairs. The amount of the mortgage is based on the appraised value of the home "as-completed" (either the sales price plus rehabilitation costs or the appraised "as completed" value, whichever is lower). In addition, you must have cash reserves equal to two months' mortgage payments at the time of closing.

Rehabilitation cost. The repair work may represent up to 30 percent of the property's appraised value after repairs are made. The cost of rehabilitation is determined by rehabilitation plans, specifications, and a licensed contractor's itemized estimate for all work. The rehabilitation must be performed by licensed contractors.

Rehabilitation escrow account. The funds needed for the rehabilitation are held by the lender in an insured, interest-bearing special deposit (escrow) account. With the lender's approval, you withdraw funds from the rehabilitation escrow account as needed to pay for the work. The lender is responsible for administering this account and assuring that the repairs and rehabilitation are completed according to the plans and specifications.

Other Mortgage Options

Housing finance agency assistance. States and many localities have agencies known as "housing finance agencies" that make mortgage money available at below-market interest rates. Contact your state or local housing finance agency by checking the telephone directory "blue pages" or call your local housing department.

Are you ready for homeownership?

Having read this opening chapter, perhaps you will conclude that you are not ready for homeownership today, but you may be able to buy a house within a couple of years.

To help decide whether you are in a good position to buy a house, ask yourself the following questions:

❑ Are you sure you want to buy a house?
❑ Do you have steady income and stable employment?
❑ Do you anticipate remaining in the same geographic location for the next couple of years?
❑ Have you created a budget so you know how

much more you can realistically afford to pay for housing?
❑ Do you have an established credit record or can you build a nontraditional credit history with records of payments to previous landlords, utility companies, cable television companies, insurance companies? If so, is your credit profile favorable? Do you pay your bills on time?
❑ Do you have enough money saved up for a down payment and closing costs? If not, can you enlist the aid of relatives or government or nonprofit agencies?
❑ Have you been "prequalified" by a lender so you know how much you can borrow based on your income and existing debt?
❑ Is your existing debt low enough that it will not limit your ability to qualify for a mortgage? If not, can you pay down your debt before you attempt to buy a house?
❑ Have you looked into the benefits and requirements of the numerous mortgage products that are now available to low- and moderate-income homebuyers?
❑ Have you attended a homebuyer education seminar?

If you can answer yes to all of these questions, you may be well on your way to owning your own home!

Summary

Homeownership involves both advantages and obligations. That's why it is important to take a realistic look at whether homeownership is right for you. By analyzing your current expenses and comparing them to the up-front and ongoing costs of a home purchase, you can determine whether you can afford to buy a house. This chapter has suggested resources for your down payment and closing costs and the guidelines lenders use to determine loan amounts. It has also described ways you can increase your borrowing power, including financing options for low- and moderate-income homebuyers. The next chapter will explain how to decide which features in a house are most important to you and how to find a house that is both affordable and meets your needs.

CHAPTER 2

Shopping for a Home

Overview

After you have considered how much money you can put toward a down payment and how large a mortgage you can qualify for, you will have a good idea of your price range and you can begin shopping for a home. This chapter explains what that process involves. We begin with why it is important to think about what location, size, style, and special features you're looking for. We then suggest ways to locate a house that is both affordable and offers the features you want. Next, we focus on how to negotiate the purchase price. The chapter closes with an explanation of the nature and importance of a professional home inspection. In the course of this chapter, we also look at the role of three important professionals whose services you will be using: the real estate sales professional, the home inspection expert, and the settlement agent.

Your New Home

New vs. Existing Home

Eight out of 10 homebuyers purchase existing rather than new homes. Some people like the idea of moving into a brand new house, but many prefer older homes.

If you're handy with tools, you may be willing to consider a house that needs work (what real estate ads call a "handyman's special" or "fixer upper"). Or, you may insist on a house that is in perfect condition. Most homebuyers fall somewhere between these two extremes, and even finicky buy-

ers often decide to accept some imperfections when they see the price of perfection.

New houses are typically clustered together in areas where the sizes, styles, and prices are very similar. New homes are likely to have more efficient heating systems, may be better insulated, and should cost less to maintain than older homes. Older homes, on the other hand, may be larger, more individual, or made with better-quality materials.

Location

For many people, the location of the home they buy is their most important consideration; for many others, location may not be a real choice. You probably know already whether you will be looking in an urban, suburban, or rural area. You may already know what neighborhood you want to live in.

Choosing a neighborhood...
Consider what's important to you—do you need to find a house near your job site, public services, or day-care facilities, or can you commute some distance to and from work in order to live in a house with a yard? Are neighborhood schools a major factor in your home-buying decision? Is proximity to shopping, recreational activities, or public transportation particularly important? Also, make sure to check with the local community government's tax office to see what the annual taxes and fees are for similar houses in the community. Much of this information can be found online, but a quick phone call can often achieve the best results.

Size Requirements

In choosing a home, an important consideration is the number and size of rooms. Is the house the right size for your family? Will your family soon outgrow it? Will you be paying for more house than you need? The amount of land on which the house sits, or the size of the lot, also will influence the price of a house. If space for a yard, garden, or off-street parking is important to you, this will narrow your options.

In determining what size house to buy, you need to consider both your current and future housing needs. You will want to look for a house that will be adequate for at least the next five to 15 years.

Special Features

You also should think about whether there are any special features in a home that would be particularly important to you and your family. Make a list of "must haves" and "would likes." Is a garage a necessity? A second or third bathroom? A porch? Air conditioning? Wheelchair accessibility? You may not find a house in your price range with everything you want, but it helps to tell a real estate sales professional what features are most important. Many have Web sites where you can search for properties by feature, size, price, and location.

Special Types of Houses

The type of neighborhood you want to live in will have considerable bearing on the available style of house, whether it is a single-family detached house, a townhouse, or a unit in a condominium or cooperative project. Let's look briefly at some of the nontraditional housing choices.

Condominiums...

Condominiums are the "starter home" of choice for many homebuyers today because they are generally smaller and less expensive than conventional single-family houses. The term "condominium" does not describe a particular style of architecture, but rather a type of joint ownership. Each living unit is individually owned while the facilities and common space (the surrounding land, the hallways and elevators, and any recreational facilities) are owned collectively by the owners of each unit. In addition to their monthly mortgage payment, condominium owners pay a "condo fee" for the management of the complex, upkeep of the common property areas, and occasionally some utilities.

Condominiums combine some of the advantages (and disadvantages) of apartment living with those of homeownership. Condominium owners reap the same financial benefits (tax breaks and equity build-up) as other homeowners without many of the traditional chores of homeownership, such as shoveling the walk and hiring a contractor to fix the leaky roof. Moreover, condos often offer such amenities as landscaping, meeting rooms, and recreation rooms. Many are in planned communities offering wooded areas and ample play space.

Selecting a condominium is more complex than buying a single-family home; you need to investigate not only the specific unit in which you are interested, but also the entire project, from a physical and financial standpoint.

A townhouse condominium is simply another type of condominium in which units of two or more stories share common walls. Each unit has its own ground space, but like other condominiums, the common spaces and facilities are collectively owned by all the unit owners.

Cooperatives (Co-ops)...

Co-ops resemble condominiums in that they owned by a collective. However, legally they are different. Co-op owners have shares in a corporation that owns the property rather than owning the individual units in which they live. Cooperatives are a well-established form of ownership in New York City and some other parts of the country.

Planned unit developments (PUDs)...

A planned unit development is a project or subdivision that consists of common property that is owned and maintained by an owners' association for the benefit and use of the individual PUD unit owners.

Manufactured housing...
Most new homes in the United States are site-built to state and local codes, but an increasing number are "manufactured housing." They are factory-built or pre-fabricated housing, including mobile homes.

Finding the "Right" House

How do you start the search for a house that you can afford and that comes closest to meeting your needs? The first step is to identify houses on the market.

Sources of Leads

To find the right house, check as many leads as possible. Consider the following sources.

Word of mouth...
Now is the time to let all your friends and acquaintances know that you're looking to buy a house. If you get lucky, you may hear of houses that are just coming on the market.

"For sale" signs...
Driving or walking around in search of "for sale" signs may be worthwhile, particularly if you have a good idea of what neighborhood you are interested in. This is a particularly good way to find houses that are being sold by the owner.

Newspaper ads...
Classified ads in local newspapers are another good source of leads. "Open houses" also are announced in the real estate section, and you can do some initial shopping and comparative pricing by spending weekend afternoons looking at houses displayed by real estate sales professionals.

Shoppers' guides...
Home finders' directories with pictures and descriptions of houses on the market may be available at newsstands, convenience stores, or supermarkets, especially in metropolitan areas.

Internet...
Home listings are also available on the Internet. Many Web sites have the advantage of allowing you to specify the location, size, and price range of the homes in which you are interested.

How a Real Estate Sales Professional Can Help

Although these sources will get you started, perhaps the most efficient method of shopping for a house is to consult a real estate sales professional. How do you select a real estate sales professional and what services can you expect?

If you know someone who has recently bought a house, ask for a referral. Try to find an experienced agent or broker who works primarily in the area where you are interested in purchasing a home and who has access to a computerized multiple listing service (MLS), an automated system for generating a list of houses that match your requirements. Make sure that the real estate professional is a member of the National Association of Realtors® by checking www.realtor.org and is identified as a Realtor®. Your local Yellow Pages are also a good place to check for a real estate professional.

The relationship between a homebuyer and a real estate sales professional is unusual in that you usually pay nothing for the agent's services. Instead, agents are paid by the sellers (usually a commission based on the sales price of the home) and often represent the seller's interest in the transaction.

In many areas of the country, it may be possible to locate a real estate sales professional who will act as a buyer's agent—that is, who will represent your interests. However, you should determine how the buyer's agent will be paid. Will you be charged a commission? Or will the buyer's agent split the seller-paid commission with the seller's agent?

A real estate sales professional can provide you with a broad range of services including the following:

- Use your wish list to generate a computer print-out of houses that meet your specifications.
- Show you houses that meet your requirements.
- Provide you with information about a community, including the prices and characteristics of

houses in the area, the location of schools, property tax rates, unusual building code regulations, and availability of community services.

- Present your offer to the seller.
- Advise you on mortgage lenders, real estate settlement agents, professional home inspectors, and title companies.

Here are some tips for working successfully with a real estate sales professional. These are particularly important if you use a buyer's agent.

- Interview the real estate sales professional before you start home hunting. This person will play an important role in the purchase of your home, so it is vital that you understand what you can expect from them. Good real estate sales professionals will spend time answering your questions. If they don't, think about choosing a different one.
- If you decided to use a particular real estate sales professional, it usually makes sense not to work with others. As the real estate sales professional most likely will work hardest for those clients for whom they are the exclusive agent.
- Many real estate sales professionals will ask you to sign a limited-term exclusive agent agreement to ensure that you do not switch real estate sales professionals part way through the process, read the agreement carefully so you are comfortable with it before signing.
- It's in your best interest to look at as many houses as possible. Be specific about what you're looking for (by completing Worksheet 6, page 77) to make the best use of your time and the real estate sales professionals.
- If you feel you are being steered to (or away from) particular neighborhoods, you should report your grievance to the U.S. Department of Housing and Urban Development (HUD), the agency in charge of enforcing the Fair Housing Act. The Fair Housing Act prohibits discrimination on the basis of race, religion, age, color, national origin, receipt of public assistance funds, sex, or marital status. You may also want to file a complaint concerning that agent with your local Board of Realtors® as well as your local HUD office.

Comparison Shopping

A recent survey showed that on the average, homebuyers look at 15 houses before settling on one. Comparison shopping is an essential part of the home-buying process, so approach it objectively and consider these pointers.

Keeping records...
Once you start looking at houses, it won't be long before they become a blur in your mind. For this reason it's helpful to keep records of all the houses you see. You want to be able to compare features and prices of the various houses you have seen. Using a preprinted form such as Worksheet 7 (page 79), "House evaluation checklist," may help you stay organized and remind you of things you will want to recall about each house.

Include the observations about the interior and exterior of each house, including your first impressions. Make sure that you are judging the house itself and not the furnishings. A digital camera is a great tool for this process.

What to look for...
Train yourself to look critically at every house. Rate houses based on your own needs. Don't be afraid to ask questions of the real estate sales professional and the owners, and expect satisfactory, straightforward answers.

The neighborhood. The amount you are willing to pay for a house may be affected by the nature of the community. Is it a designated historic district, and if so will you be bound by any regulations? Are many houses for sale in the area? If so, why? Are there plans underway to change the zoning regulations? How will that affect the neighborhood? Is it convenient to public transportation? Shopping? Recreational facilities? Schools? Are there renters in the neighborhood?

Physical details. Start with what is visible from the outside: the size and age of the house, its structural condition and outside maintenance, the size of the lot, and landscaping. Inside, you might want to sketch the floor plan. How many rooms and baths are on each floor? Is there adequate storage space? Is the basement finished? What built-in appliances are there? Is the kitchen functional? Is there central or room air-conditioning? Does the basement flood or the roof leak?

Construction details. Whether the house is new or old, the quality of the building materials and the craftsmanship and the condition are important considerations. How well insulated is it? Are the windows energy efficient? Is the roof in good condition? Does the house appear to have been well maintained? Does the foundation appear to be in good shape? Are there low spots in the yard where water might drain improperly?

Major systems. Are the plumbing, heating and cooling, and electrical systems in good working order? Or does the house need to be rewired and replumbed and a new furnace installed? What type of fuel is used for heating and what is the approximate cost per month and year? How much do the other monthly utilities cost?

Financing. The MLS printout provided by the real estate sales professional will include the asking price and also may include the mortgage balance, the seller's monthly payments, whether the mortgage is assumable and, if relevant, how large a second mortgage the seller is willing to take back. If a low-interest rate mortgage is part of your house-buying strategy, the seller's current financing will be an important consideration for you.

Narrowing the field...
Plan to spend enough time looking at houses so that you have a good idea of the market. After you've looked at a number of houses, you will get a feel for what's available in various neighborhoods and which areas you prefer. The more houses you look at, the easier it is to determine whether the asking price is high or low.

When you find a house that you like in your price range, you will still want to proceed carefully and calmly. No matter how "perfect" the house may seem, don't make a decision without going back at least once to take a closer look. Visit the neighbor-

hood at different times on different days—are weekday evenings as quiet as Sunday afternoons? Chat with your prospective neighbors. Avoid the temptation to jump into a deal for fear that another buyer will grab it while you're investigating. You should never sign any papers or put any money down on a house without careful consideration.

Negotiating the Purchase

Deciding How Much to Offer

In deciding how much you should offer, there are a number of factors to consider.

Market value of the house...
How does the asking price compare to the market value of the house based on recent sales of comparable houses in the area? To find out, ask whether the listing agent prepared a comparative market analysis (CMA) on the property. This is a written report that reviews prices of comparable homes on the market, under contract, and that have sold in the past several months.

Condition of the house...
Before making an offer, you should be aware of major problems with the house. You should have inspected the house and questioned the sales agent and the owner about the structural soundness and condition of the basic systems. Both sellers and real estate sales professionals can be held liable if they fail to tell the buyer of any known defects. You should also have a clear idea of what it will cost to fix any major problems of which you are aware.

If you are buying an existing house rather than a new house, a home inspection by a professional should be one of the contingencies in your sales contract. We will return to this topic later in this chapter.

Circumstances surrounding the sale...
In deciding how much to offer, try to determine how anxious the owners are to sell. For example, if the sellers already have a contract on another house that is dependent on the sale of this house,

you may be in a good negotiating position. It will be to your advantage to know how long the house has been on the market and whether the asking price has already been reduced. Also, how much did the seller pay for the house and when? And how much equity does the seller have in the property? Agents usually can obtain this information.

What you can afford...

Before making an offer on a house, you need to know what your monthly housing costs (PITI) at the price you plan to offer. This requires knowing the annual cost of utilities, local taxes, homeowner's insurance, condominium fee (if applicable), and any special assessments, as well as the current rate for whatever mortgage loan product you are considering. Make sure the amount of your down payment is adequate and you have enough to cover the closing costs. Don't be tempted to offer more than you can afford.

Financing terms...

Remember that there are two aspects to an offer—the price and the financing terms. The terms may actually be more important to you than the price. For example, if the seller is willing to offer attractive financing terms, including paying for the title search, the home inspection, and other settlement costs, you may be more willing to accept the price. The real estate sales professional will be glad to advise you as to how much you should offer. However, the decision is yours alone. (Remember, the agent typically acts on behalf of the seller.) Most prospective buyers do not offer the full asking price, at least initially. For example, you may want to offer less than the asking price if you feel that the condition of the house warrants a lower price.

Submitting the Offer

You make an offer by submitting to the real estate sales professional a signed offer to purchase the house for a given price under specified terms. This document is called a "purchase and sale agreement." You may want to explain in detail to the agent that your price reflects certain flaws that you noted during your inspection of the house. The agent is required by law to deliver your offer to the seller.

Earnest money...

This is a "good faith" payment you submit with the offer to show the seller that you are serious. There is no set amount that is required, and what is customary differs by location. The check should not be made out to the seller directly. Rather, it may be made out to the brokerage firm of the real estate sales professional. The earnest money should be deposited in escrow to be returned to you if the seller does not accept your offer within a specified number of days. You usually forfeit the money if the seller accepts the contract and then you back out of the deal.

What the offer includes...

The offer to purchase should include at least the following:

*   A complete legal description of the property;
*   The amount of earnest money accompanying the offer;
*   The price you are offering;
*   The size of your down payment and how the remainder of the purchase will be financed (including the maximum interest rate you are willing to pay);
*   Any items of personal property the owner has said will stay with the house or that you want to be included;
*   A proposed closing date and occupancy date;
*   Length of time the offer is valid (three to five days); and
*   The satisfaction of contingencies.

Terms of the Contract

In addition to the basic terms of the sale, certain "contingencies" may be included in the contract. These are conditions that must be met in order for the contract to take effect. Some contingencies and other provisions that are commonly written in a contract are summarized here.

Financing contingency...

The contract should state the purchase price, the amount of down payment, the total loan amount, and the financing terms you will accept—as well as how long you have to find the agreed-upon financing. It also will state the amount of deposit being held in escrow and which closing costs are to be paid by the buyer and which by the seller.

This contingency makes clear that if you don't get the money you need at the terms you have specified, the deal is off and your deposit will be refunded. The seller in turn may insist that a clause be included requiring you to make a "good-faith effort" to obtain the mortgage.

Inspection contingencies...

As we noted earlier, unless you are buying a new home, it is highly recommended the house be inspected by a professional. You may also want to specify that certain inspections are completed before the sales contract takes effect.

Professional home inspections. Your contract should be contingent on a satisfactory report by a professional home inspector. If any major problems with the structure or systems of the house are uncovered, you have the right to back out of the purchase or to re-negotiate the terms of the purchase. We will explore this topic in more detail later in this chapter.

Termites. It is standard practice to require the seller to pay for a termite inspection and to provide a written certification stating that the property is free of termite infestation and that any damage from past infestation has been repaired.

Environmental hazards to investigate...

Radon. Many homebuyers today insist that the house be tested for the presence of radon, a naturally occurring, odorless gas that can seep into houses and cause major health problems. For more information about radon in your area, call your state or county public health department.

- The Indoor Air Quality Information Clearinghouse (IAQ INFO) is an easily accessible, central source of information on indoor air quality created and supported by the U.S. Environmental Protection Agency (EPA). IAQ INFO at (800) 438-4318 to speak to an information specialist, Monday through Friday, 9 a.m. to 5 p.m. Eastern time.

- The National Hispanic Indoor Air Quality Hotline provides bilingual (Spanish/English) information about indoor air pollutants that consumers may find inside their homes, offices, or schools. Hotline staff can be reached at (800) 725-8312 from Monday through Friday, 9 a.m. to 6 p.m. Eastern time.

Lead-based paint. If the house was built before 1950, you can be almost certain that lead-based paint was used. For houses built after 1950 but before 1978, there is a fair chance that lead-based paint is present. The presence of lead paint should be investigated because even low levels of lead exposure can have very serious health, intelligence, and behavioral consequences, especially for infants, young children, and pregnant women. Children do not have to eat lead-based paint chips to be poisoned. Lead-contaminated dust on children's hands and toys can pass into their mouths.

Before a sales contract on a home built before 1978 can be finalized, the seller (or his/her agent) must give you a pamphlet discussing lead hazards in the home and tell you about any lead-based paint or lead-based paint hazards of which they are aware. Sellers must also allow you 10 days to hire a trained professional to conduct an inspection or risk assessment of lead-based paint hazards. You can make the sales contract contingent on this lead hazard evaluation. Find an inspector or risk assessor who has taken an EPA course or is certified in your state. A lead paint inspection will tell you what surfaces are coated with lead paint. A risk assessment will identify any lead hazards—such as peeling paint or contaminated dust—and what steps are needed to correct them.

Renovation projects on older homes can disturb lead-based paint and be particularly dangerous. Don't attempt lead-based paint removal projects yourself.

The National Lead Information Center (NLIC) is operated by the Environmental Health Center, a division of the nongovernmental, not-for-profit National Safety Council.

To receive a general information packet, order other documents, or for information, call the center's clearinghouse and speak with a specialist at (800) 424-LEAD, Monday through Friday, 8:30 a.m. to 6 p.m. Eastern time.

Asbestos. According to the EPA, many homes constructed in the past 20 years probably do not contain asbestos products. You may hire a qualified professional trained and experienced in working with asbestos to inspect the home. A professional knows where to look for asbestos, how to take samples properly, and what corrective actions will be most effective.

Formaldehyde. Formaldehyde is a colorless, gaseous chemical compound emitted by many construction materials and was also an ingredient in foam used for home insulating until the early 1980s. It can cause irritation of the eyes, nose, and throat and is suspected of causing cancer. In new homes, check with the builder on whether construction materials containing formaldehyde were used. A qualified building inspector can examine the home for formaldehyde-emitting materials. Home monitoring kits also are available.

Hazardous waste sites. Generally, testing for hazardous waste involves skills and technology not available to the average homeowner or home-remodeling contractor. The EPA has identified more than 30,000 potentially contaminated waste sites nationwide. Contact the nearest regional EPA office for information on the location and status of hazardous waste sites.

Mold Infiltration. Mold is an increasingly dangerous problem for homeowners. Make sure your housing inspection covers this topic. For more information, visit www.epa.gov/mold/moldresources.html.

Appraisal contingency...
When applying for a loan, the lender will require a professional appraisal of the property's market value. The appraised value of the house determines how large a mortgage the lender will give you. If the appraised value is lower than the agreed-upon purchase price, this contingency gives you the right to withdraw your offer.

Other provisions...
You also may want to include certain other provisions in the contract so nothing is left to chance.

Repair work. You may want to stipulate that the sellers are responsible for ensuring that the plumbing, heating, mechanical, and electrical systems are in working order at closing. Without this clause, you agree to accept the house "as is." You also should conduct a walk-through inspection of the house on the day of settlement or several days before to determine if all conditions in the contract have been satisfied.

Personal property. Don't rely on the seller's verbal agreement that specific fixtures, appliances, and personal property are included in the sale. To avoid any misunderstandings or surprises, list in the contract everything that the owner is supposed to leave behind.

Closing and occupancy date. You may want to include a provision that the seller must pay you rent on a daily basis in the event they haven't moved out by the agreed-upon date (usually the closing date).

Clear title. The contract should state that the purchase is subject to your receiving clear title to the property. The title search and title insurance will be discussed in Chapter 4.

Negotiating the final purchase price...
The seller may respond to your offer in one of three ways: by accepting it, by rejecting it (in which case you must decide whether to make another offer), or by making their own suggestion, known as a counter offer. Always take your time in considering a counter offer.

Typically the real estate sales professional will present your offer to the seller and will relay the seller's response back to you. Negotiating the final purchase price is usually accomplished in much the same way. You may be expected to put a larger deposit down (to be held in escrow) once the seller has signed your offer. You need not, however, tie up the entire amount of your down payment at this point.

The Home Inspection

As we noted previously, one of the contingencies in your contract should be that you obtain a satisfactory home inspection report. You will, of course, have examined the house to the best of your ability before making an offer on it. But before you go through with the purchase, you will want an expert to take a critical look at the property. Although you will pay for this inspection, it is well worth the cost in peace of mind. In a "hot" housing market, your real estate sales professional may suggest that you not include an inspection contingency in your contract for fear of losing the house to other buyers. If you follow this advice, be aware of the additional risk you are taking on.

Finding a Qualified Inspector

The NFCC recommends that you contact the American Society of Home Inspectors, which sets rigorous standards for its members. To obtain the names of local members of this organization, contact (800) 743-2744. You can expect to pay $150 to $200 for an inspection, including a written report (not just a checklist) within one or two days. You also can check your local Yellow Pages for Building Inspection Services. Always ask for three recent referrals from clients. Some states maintain online registries of home inspectors licensed to operate in the state or those who have received additional training or certification. Another good source referral source is your state weatherization program inspectors. Contact your state department of energy for more information or visit www.eere.energy.gov/weatherization.

What the Inspection Includes

A home inspection is not the same as an appraisal. The inspection is meant to evaluate the structural and mechanical condition (not the market value) of the property. The inspector's findings will be based on observable, unconcealed structural conditions. The inspector will not normally guarantee or warrant the condition of the home or determine whether a house is in compliance with local building codes.

It is strongly recommended that you accompany the inspector on his or her rounds. You can expect the inspection to take about two hours. You will undoubtedly pick up valuable maintenance tips along the way, get a chance to ask questions, and learn more about the extent of possible problems. You also will be in a better position to understand the written report.

Every inspection should include an evaluation of at least the following:

- Foundations
- Doors and windows
- Roof and siding
- Plumbing and electrical systems
- Heating and air conditioning systems
- Ceilings, walls, and floors
- Insulation
- Ventilation
- Septic tanks, wells, or sewer lines
- Common areas (in the case of a condominium or cooperative)

Using the Inspection Report

The inspector's report will not include a recommendation as to whether you should buy the house, nor will it evaluate the purchase price. If major flaws are uncovered, it should give you some idea of what the repair or replacement costs. A reputable home inspector will never offer to perform needed repairs and should not refer you to a contractor to perform such repairs.

An inspection report may serve the following purposes:

- Identify problems before you purchase a home to prevent unpleasant surprises later;

- Enable you to get out of a purchase agreement (and get your deposit refunded) if serious problems are identified;
- Help you negotiate an adjustment in the purchase price if you want to buy the house in spite of the problems;
- Get the seller to agree to pay for needed repairs, either before or after the sale using escrowed funds; and
- Make you feel confident about going ahead with the purchase.

When you and the sellers have agreed on all the provisions of the contract, you are ready to shop for a loan. The lender will want to see a copy of the signed contract when you apply for the mortgage. (For more on shopping for a mortgage, see Chapter 3.)

Summary

Shopping for a home takes time and hard work, but the effort is worth it if you find a home that's right for you. As this chapter has shown, the first step is to determine your price range and housing needs. You are then in a good position to follow up on leads and work with a real estate sales professional who can show you homes on the market, present your offer to the seller, and advise you regarding mortgage lenders, real estate settlement agents, title companies, and professional home inspectors. When you have located the house you want, it's time to negotiate the purchase price and sales contract and hire a professional home inspector. If you reach an agreement with the seller on the final purchase price and the terms of the contract (including any contingencies), the next step is to obtain financing—and that is the subject of the following chapter.

CHAPTER 3

Obtaining a Mortgage

Overview

Most homebuyers have to rely on their borrowing power to buy a house. This chapter explains how to go about obtaining a mortgage. We begin by listing the sources of mortgage loans and explaining how to search for a lender that offers the most attractive terms on mortgage loans. We also provide a checklist that will help you shop for a loan by comparing terms being offered by different lenders. We then look at the loan application process itself, including what to expect from a loan interview and the procedures lenders follow in determining whether or not to approve a loan. Finally, we look at some alternatives you may want to consider if your loan application is turned down.

Shopping for a Loan

Shopping for a mortgage that meets your particular needs is not an easy job, but it is an inescapable part of the process of buying a home. By now, you may have done some preliminary research on interest rates and gone through the process of "prequalifying" for a loan. If you requested a credit report and resolved any problems in your record, or if you assembled documentation on your nontraditional credit history, you can now shop for a mortgage with confidence.

Your challenge is to select loan terms that are most favorable to your situation. For example, if you anticipate that you will be living for many years in the house you are buying now, the interest rate

may be your primary consideration. If you anticipate keeping the house for only two or three years, the closing costs and whether or not there is a prepayment penalty (a charge for repaying the loan early) may be more important to you.

By the time you have a signed sales contract, you should have a clear idea of what kind of financing you need or want. Now you need to shop around for the lender that offers the best terms for that type of loan. You may be surprised at the range of interest rates quoted, as well as the considerable variation in the fees charged by lenders for originating and processing a loan application.

Even if you have already been prequalified by a lender, you should satisfy yourself that the rates and loan terms offered by that lender compare favorably with those of other lenders. It's definitely worth your while to shop around!

Sources of Mortgage Loans

Mortgages are available from a number of sources including:

- Savings and loan associations;
- Commercial banks;
- Mortgage companies;
- Federal credit unions; and
- Financial companies.

You might do well to start your search for a mortgage with a financial institution with which you already have a financial relationship, such as a checking or savings accounts. Contact your local financial institution or check out its Web site to see if it offers home mortgages, and if so, whether it grants favorable terms to its own account holders. If you are a member of a federal credit union, you should investigate whether it makes home loans.

Your real estate sales professional may know which lenders in your area are offering the best terms. Also, ask friends, family, or co-workers for recommendations. Some people prefer using the services of a mortgage broker who will shop your loan application to various lenders around the country. This process can save you time, but make sure that the fees paid are equal to the services provided.

Your local newspaper is also a good source of information. Check the real estate section to review the comparative mortgage rate charts. Your local area also might have a mortgage rate hotline in your area.

Shopping by the telephone...
To begin with, plan to contact lenders at a half dozen or more companies (of different kinds) that offer home mortgages in your area.

Shopping via the Internet...
Increasing numbers of lenders have Web sites allowing borrowers to shop for mortgages online. In addition, there are many mortgage brokers that allow you to choose from a number of lenders and in many cases you can make a formal loan application online.

It is important to remember that making a loan application online is a serious step, as it is exactly the same as making one with a loan officer in a financial institution, so we strongly recommend that you avoid making applications to "test the market" if you know you are not really ready to buy. Unfortunately some borrowers have made many applications for mortgages over an extended period and have found that this has had a negative effect on their credit score.

Comparing Loan Terms

Comparing loan terms among various lenders can be a confusing process, unless you approach it systematically. Use Worksheet 8 (page 81), "Mortgage terms checklist," to make sure you get all of the information you need to compare the various lenders' policies and terms. Make several copies of this worksheet and use it as a guide when you call loan officers to compare terms.

Mortgage terms checklist...
To help you better understand the various mortgage terms available, we will discuss each item on the checklist in turn.

Types of mortgages available. Begin by telling the loan officer what type of loan you are interested in—for example, a 95 percent 30-year fixed-rate mortgage. (If you plan to make a down payment of 5 percent of the purchase price, lenders call this a "95 percent loan.") If you're shopping for an adjustable-rate mortgage (ARM), you will want to ask about a one-year, three-year, or five-year ARM (the number of years indicates the period for which the interest rate will be fixed).

For some homebuyers, an important decision is whether a fixed-rate or adjustable-rate mortgage is preferable. As we discussed in Chapter 1, fixed-rate mortgages may be preferable to ARMs because your monthly principal and interest payment is fixed for the life of the loan (though your tax and insurance payments may change over time). However, ARMs usually offer a lower initial interest rate, which means lower initial monthly principal and interest payments, and the possibility of qualifying for a larger mortgage amount. If you're confident that your income will increase steadily over the years, you may have no qualms about an ARM. Again, consider your own circumstances.

If you are interested in one or more of the mortgage products designed for low- and moderate-income families described in Chapter 1, or in FHA or VA financing, ask whether the lender handles these loans. You will want to be sure that you are comparing terms among various lenders for exactly the same type of loan, so be specific.

Interest rate. Lenders change their rates often, even daily. In addition, the same lender will quote different rates for each specific type of loan it offers. The interest rate you get will not only determine how large a mortgage you qualify for (as we saw in Chapter 1), but the size of your monthly payments. Even a quarter of a percent difference in the interest rate represents a lot of money over the term of a 30-year loan.

In order to accurately compare the rates quoted by different lenders, you also need to know how many "points" the lender will charge.

Origination fees (points). Lenders typically charge a loan origination fee in the form of points. Each point is equal to 1 percent of the loan amount. For example, one point on a $100,000 mortgage would be $1000. Points are usually paid as a one-time expense at closing.

Paying additional points can lower your interest rate (discount points). Some borrowers may wish to pay additional fees to the lender in order to lower the interest rate. That is why you will see a lender offering rate and point combinations of, for example, 8 percent and 2 points or 8.25 percent and 0 points. The more points you pay at closing, the lower your interest rate should be.

Annual percentage rate (APR). To compare easily the various combinations of interest rates and number of points that lenders quote, ask for the APR of a particular mortgage. This is the actual interest rate taking into account the points and other costs of financing.

Long term. Find out the longest maturity, or repayment period, the lender offers. Most home loans are repaid over 15 to 30 years. With a shorter repayment term, you pay less interest over the term of the loan, but your monthly payments will be higher. First-time homebuyers typically take the longest mortgage term offered in order to get the lowest possible monthly payments.

Down payment requirement. Ask what a lender's lowest allowable down payment is—with and without private mortgage insurance

Private mortgage insurance (PMI). If mortgage insurance will be required, how much will it cost? Ask about the up-front cost (payable at closing) and monthly premiums. All private mortgage insurance companies now offer programs that don't require up-front payment at closing, though the monthly premium may be slightly higher. FHA loans also require an up-front mortgage insurance payment, known as Mortgage Insurance Premium (MIP).

Canceling mortgage insurance. Once a borrower has built up sufficient equity in the home, most can cancel the mortgage insurance premium and lower the monthly payment. Canceling mortgage insurance has become much easier. Under federal law, PMI on most loans originated on or after July 29, 1999, will terminate automatically once the mortgage has amortized to 78 percent of the original purchase price and the borrower is current on all mortgage payments. The lender must tell the borrower at closing when the mortgage will hit 78 percent. The process is slightly different for FHA loans made after January 1, 2001. In that case, the MIP automatically will be canceled once the unpaid principal balance, excluding the up-front MIP, reaches 78 percent of the initial sales price or appraised value, whichever is lower.

There are exceptions to these rules. Ask your lender at what point you can cancel your mortgage insurance.

Credit Insurance: A word of warning...
Credit Insurance protects homebuyers if they default on a loan. It is up to the consumer to decide whether they wish to buy such a policy.

However, paying for the whole policy up-front as a part of closing is almost never a good idea. By borrowing the money as part of the mortgage, which you will pay interest on, you are buying a 30-year non-refundable insurance policy and paying the insurance company all 30 years of payments in advance. Although the lender involved makes a significant commission by selling the policy, we believe that it makes very little sense for the homebuyer.

If your lender tells you that credit insurance is required, ask to have this requirement in writing and seek the help of a housing counselor immediately.

Rate lock-in. When a lender quotes you an interest rate, that is the rate in effect today, but it may not be the rate available to you when you actually close the loan. Since a higher interest rate may reduce the size of the mortgage for which you qualify, it's important for you to know whether a lender will agree to hold the quoted rate for you. This is called a "lock-in." A lock-in may save you thousands of dollars in interest over the life of the loan.

As interest rates change daily you should be very clear about how the lock-in works. Some of the questions you should ask are these: If the lender will lock in a rate when will it do so, at the time of application or only upon approval? Will the lender lock in both the interest rate and points? Can you get a written lock-in agreement? How long does the lock-in remain in effect? Is there a charge for locking in a rate? If the rate drops before closing, can you lock in at a lower rate?

Prepayments. Some lenders charge borrowers a prepayment penalty if they pay the loan off early. Unless you think you won't sell your house before the loan is paid off (the majority of mortgages are repaid within seven years) and won't refinance your loan should rates drop, look for a loan with no prepayment penalty.

Escrow requirement. Generally, the lender will include the cost of property taxes and insurance in your monthly payment. Ask the lender how much will be escrowed each month and whether you will earn interest on the amount.

Processing time. How long does this lender normally take to process a loan application?

Traditionally, loan approvals have taken 30 to 60 days or more. Some lenders now promise very short approval times (some within 24 hours thanks to automated under-writing), which may be an advantage, especially in times of rising interest rates or if you are particularly anxious to complete the purchase and move.

Closing costs. Many of the closing costs are fees imposed by the lender, which may vary considerably from one lender to the next. Ask specifically about the following: the application fee, origination fee, credit report fee, appraisal fee, survey (if one is required), fees for the lender's attorney, cost of title search and title insurance, and document preparation fee. If you plan to assume an existing mortgage, what is the assumption fee? (Many if not all of these fees can be negotiated with lenders, so be sure you understand what each fee is for and if it seems high ask your lender why.)

Payment schedule. Normally borrowers make one payment a month, or 12 payments a year. With a biweekly payment plan, you make payments every other week, or 26 payments a year. If you get paid twice a month, rather than once a month, you may want to consider a payment schedule that matches your pay period. It will save you a surprising amount of interest over the life of the loan.

Adjustable-rate mortgage (ARM) checklist...
If you are shopping for an adjustable-rate mortgage, you want an ARM that offers you the best protection in the event of skyrocketing interest rates. The most important thing to find out is the maximum amount your payments would increase. Would you be able to make such payments? (See "Mortgage terms checklist," Worksheet 8, page 81) The following information will help you compare ARMs offered by various lenders.

Initial interest rate. Watch out for "introductory discount" or "teaser" rates, in which a lender offers very low initial rates. They may appear to be a bargain, but remember that the low rates last only until the first adjustment. After that you will be charged the full rate, at which point your payments may become unmanageable. Such loans may cost more than a standard ARM in the long run.

Adjustment interval. Find out how often the interest rate will be adjusted: annually? Every three years? Every five years? A loan with an adjustment period of one year is called a "one-year ARM", the interest rate and monthly payment change once every year.

Financial index and margin. What financial index is used to determine the interest rate? Many ARMs are pegged to U.S. Treasury notes, which are widely published in newspapers, making them easy to track. How much has this index changed in the past five years? Does the interest rate you pay come down if the financial index falls?

The margin is the rate added to the financial index to calculate your mortgage interest rate at each adjustment. What margin is the lender charging?

Rate caps. These limit how much the interest rate on an ARM can increase or decrease. Periodic caps limit the increase or decrease per adjustment period, whereas a lifetime cap limits the amount the rate can increase over the entire life of the loan. For example, the lender may stipulate that the interest rate on an ARM can increase up to 2 percent a year but not more than 5 percent over the life of the loan. A lifetime cap provides you with the most protection, but look for an ARM that offers both types of rate caps.

Payment caps. Don't confuse rate caps with payment caps. With a payment cap, there is a limit on how much your monthly principal and interest payments can increase, regardless of how high the interest rate rises. As a result, you may end up paying the lender less than the amount of interest you owe each month. The lender doesn't just forget about this. Instead, any unpaid interest is added to your loan balance. The result is that the amount you owe on your mortgage increases rather than decreases with each payment—a phenomenon called "negative amortization."

You might eventually owe the lender more than the original amount you borrowed, despite having made all monthly payments! Moreover, if your mortgage limits the amount of negative amortization that can build up, your monthly payments could increase beyond their normal cap if you reach that limit. If you agree to a mortgage with a payment cap, be sure you discuss the possible consequences with the lender.

Convertibility. Some ARMs include a provision allowing conversion to a fixed-rate mortgage at specified times, typically during the first five years of the loan. If the convertibility feature is an added expense (some lenders charge an extra point, for example), find out the exact conversion terms and how much it would cost to convert your ARM to a fixed-rate loan. This will help you decide whether this is a cost-effective option.

Other Types of Loans to Consider...
Interest Only. Interest Only loans are similar to conventional fixed rate except that only accrued interest is paid each month and the principal is paid back at the end of the interest only period.

Interest Only ARM. An Interest Only ARM only requires monthly interest payments. Since you are not paying any principal, this can lower your monthly payment. However, since your mortgage's principal balance is not decreased, you will have a balloon payment at the end of the interest only period. An Interest Only ARM will also have a maximum interest rate that it will not exceed.

Balloon. Balloons are calculated such that the monthly payment is based on the full amortization term and charged as such until the months to balloon period is reached, at which point the entire unpaid balance becomes due.

Applying for a Loan

After you have contacted several lenders, you may find that one lender is quoting the lowest interest rates but another lender charges less in up-front costs payable at closing. Perhaps yet another lender has the most favorable lock-in policy. Select the features that are most important to you. Your real estate sales professional or nonprofit housing counselor may be able to help you sort out your options.

When you have decided which lender offers the kind of mortgage you want with the best terms for your situation, make an appointment with the lender. Request that a loan application be emailed, faxed, or mailed to you and ask what documentation you should bring.

Many mortgage lenders are equipped to take loan applications over the Internet. You will need to provide the lender with the same documentation, so be prepared before submitting your application!

Plan Ahead

It is important to prepare for the loan application. Try to anticipate everything you will need and have all of the necessary information (including names, addresses with zip codes, phone numbers, dates of employment, etc.) readily available. Fill out the "Pre-application worksheet" (Worksheet 9, page 83) before you meet with the loan officer.

If you and your co-purchaser will both be signing the mortgage, you should both go to the loan interview.

Required documentation...
You will speed up the loan processing if you bring the following documents:

- The purchase contract for the house;
- Your bank account numbers, the address of your bank branch, and your latest bank statement;
- Pay stubs, W2 forms for the past two years, or other proof of employment and salary (if you are self-employed, balance sheets, tax returns for the past two years, and a year-to-date profit and loss statement);
- Information about debts, including loan and credit card numbers and names and addresses of your creditors; and
- Evidence of your mortgage or rental payments, such as canceled checks or money order receipts.

Qualification...
If you have not already been prequalified by the lender, the loan officer will first want to make sure you qualify for the loan you are applying for. As we discussed in Chapter 1, lenders traditionally have required that your monthly mortgage payment (including taxes, insurance, and condominium fee, if any) not exceed 28 percent of your gross monthly income; and that your monthly mortgage payment plus existing debt payments not exceed 36 percent of your gross monthly income. (These guidelines may be exceeded in certain circumstances—for example, with excellent credit or a substantial down payment.)

The loan application...
If you have not already done so, the lender can help you fill out the loan application. Or, you may work with a nonprofit housing counselor in reviewing your loan application. This form is designed to provide the information the lender needs to evaluate the risk involved in lending you money—the likelihood that you won't repay the loan.

Lenders speak of the "four Cs" of credit—capacity, credit history, capital, and collateral.

Capacity. Can you repay the debt? Lenders ask for employment information, including your occupation, how long you've worked, and how much you earn. They also want to know your expenses, such as how many dependents you have, whether you pay alimony or child support, and the amount of your other obligations.

Credit history. Will you repay the debt? Lenders look at your credit history: how much you owe, how often you borrow, whether you pay bills on time, and whether you live within your means.

Capital. Do you have enough cash for the down payment and for closing costs? Do you need a gift from a relative? Will you have a cushion left after your home purchase or will you spend your last penny at settlement?

Collateral. Will the lender be fully protected if you fail to repay the loan? Lenders must be sure the property you are buying is sufficient to back up your loan.

Some additional considerations. You will not help yourself by trying to cover up past credit problems. Again, it may be a good idea to ask for help from an NFCC housing counseling agency, especially if you want to assemble documents to build a nontraditional credit history.

Once you have signed the loan application, you may be bound to accept the loan if it's offered or to pay the lender's processing costs if your application is rejected. Be sure the application states amounts and terms that you find acceptable.

You may be required to pay a non-refundable application fee at this time, which typically covers the cost of the appraisal and credit report only.

Locking in the Current Rate

If you are concerned that interest rates may rise during the time the loan is being processed, the lender may agree to lock in the current rate (and number of points) for a given period. Find out when the lock-in takes effect and how long it remains in effect and get the lock-in agreement in writing. A lock-in for a short time period may be useless; you want something that will get you to closing without an extension.

Estimates of Closing Costs

Within three days after you have submitted your application for a home loan, the lender is required by law to provide you with an itemized estimate of the costs to settle (or close) the loan. This report is referred to as a "good faith estimate." The lender also must give you a copy of the government publication, Buying Your Home: Settlement Costs and Information. Read it! We will discuss the various costs in the next chapter.

Speeding up the Approval Process

Be sure to respond promptly to the lender's requests for information while your loan is being processed. It's also a good idea to call the lender occasionally to check on the status of your application. You can then contact your employer or others who need to provide documents or other information for your loan.

Loan Processing

In processing your loan application, the lender primarily will be interested in two things:

- The property that you plan to buy (since it serves as collateral for the loan); and
- Your financial situation and your credit history (since they will determine your ability and your willingness to repay the loan).

The lender will request an appraisal of the property, request a credit report on you and any co-borrowers, and verify the information in your loan application. Let's look at each of these steps.

Property Appraisal

The lender will arrange to have the property appraised, a service for which you will probably be charged. A professional appraiser will estimate the market value of the house. This information is required because the lender will loan you no more than a given percentage (often 95 percent) of the value of the property (what lenders call the "loan-to-value ratio"). If the appraised value is less than the agreed-upon purchase price, the amount of your mortgage may be smaller than anticipated and you will have a larger down payment. However, if you have included an appraisal contingency in your contract, you may be able to renegotiate the purchase price.

Credit Report

The lender also will order a credit report on you and your spouse or any other co-purchasers. The credit bureau report will show how you have handled past debt and credit accounts, such as car loans, charge accounts with stores, and any purchases made on credit. If you have recently obtained and reviewed a copy of your credit report, there should be no surprises during the loan application process. Similarly, if you provided the lender with complete documentation of your nontraditional credit history (for example, cancelled checks or receipts documenting your rental or utility payments), and this documentation demonstrates good bill-paying habits, you should be in good shape.

It is not unusual for the lender to ask you for a written explanation of any negative items that appear on your credit report. Even one late payment may require a written explanation. Don't be alarmed by this request. Just respond promptly with a truthful statement about whatever circumstances may have caused the late payment(s).

Verification

The lender also will verify the information provided on the loan application as to your income and employment history, your assets (checking and savings accounts, etc.), and your rent payment history.

Approval of Mortgage Insurer

If mortgage insurance is a requirement of the loan, the loan also will have to meet the underwriting standards of the mortgage insurer. If you are obtaining an FHA, VA, or RHS loan, the loan must also meet those standards.

Commitment Letter

When your loan is approved, the lender will send you a commitment letter. This is the formal loan offer. It will state the loan amount (the purchase price less the down payment), the term of the loan (number of years you have to repay the loan), the loan origination fee (a percentage of the loan amount), the points, the annual percentage rate or APR (the actual finance charge taking into account the interest rate and origination fees), and the monthly charges (principal and interest, taxes, and insurance, or PITI).

You will be given a set amount of time to accept the loan offer and to close the loan. Go over the commitment letter before you sign it, and be certain that you understand and will be able to comply with any conditions set by the lender. By signing the commitment letter, you accept the terms and conditions of the loan offer.

If Your Loan Application is Rejected

Having your application denied is usually an unpleasant shock, but with time and effort you will probably be able to deal with the problems that caused the denial. It is important to understand that the loan denial means that the lender is unable to approve your application with the facts they have at present, but most if not all lenders hope to get your business if and when the problems have been addressed.

Beware of people promising quick and easy solutions; you may qualify you for a different kind of loan, but pay close attention to the costs involved. Don't grab the first you can simply because you will be approved.

If your loan application is rejected, you will need to determine why so you can take steps to correct any problems or improve the likelihood of getting a future mortgage.

Understand Why the Loan was Denied

Lenders are required to explain in writing their decision to deny credit. Go back and talk to the loan officer to find out the specific reason your request was rejected. You may be able to persuade your lender to reconsider. If not, ask for suggestions of how you can improve your application. At any rate, don't assume that a rejection from one lender means rejection from other lenders.

Let's look at possible reasons for a loan denial.

Insufficient funds...
You might try to get the seller to agree to finance a second mortgage, thereby reducing the amount of down payment required. Or you could ask family members to provide funds for closing costs. Are

there local down payment or closing cost-assistance programs available? If all else fails, start a serious savings plan so you will be in a better position to buy in a year or two.

Insufficient income...

If the lender's qualifying formula shows that you can't afford the house you are proposing to buy, are there perhaps some extenuating circumstances that you might point out. For example, the rent you are already paying is as great as the proposed monthly payment. Or you may be due for a raise, which will make you eligible for the loan. You might provide a letter from your employer.

Too much debt...

Perhaps your existing debt is what's creating the roadblock. If you are close to qualifying, you may be able to convince the lender to reconsider, especially if you have an excellent credit history. Otherwise, you may need to pay off some of your debts or choose a less expensive house.

Poor credit rating...

If you are refused credit on the basis of a credit bureau report, you are entitled to a free copy of the report from the credit-reporting agency. You then can challenge any errors and insist that the credit-reporting agency include your side of any unresolved credit disputes. If your credit history is deficient in some way, start repaying debts in order to get current. Once you have improved your credit profile, you may be able to house hunt again. If you have applied for a loan using a non-traditional credit history that documents payments to landlords and utility companies, you may want to ask a nonprofit housing counseling agency to help you present the documentation in a more favorable light.

Low appraisal...

Perhaps your loan application was rejected because the appraisal of the property was too low compared to the agreed-upon purchase price. You may be able to use the low appraisal to help you renegotiate the purchase price. If the low appraisal reflects some structural problem or needed repairs, can you get the owner to fix the problem before

the sale? Or will the lender approve your loan request if the seller agrees to put funds in an escrow account to make repairs after the sale?

Seek Outside Help

Once you understand what caused the denial of your application you can develop a realistic plan for the future. Investigate state or local homeownership programs. Is the house you want to buy in an urban renewal area? If so, there may be a government program that can help you finance your purchase.

Make sure to contact an NFCC housing counseling agency for help in putting together a long-term plan for homeownership.

Investigate Alternative Financing Arrangements

As we discussed in Chapter 1, if you are a low- to moderate-income homebuyer, you will want to look into mortgage products that help homebuyers of modest means obtain affordable housing. These alternative products may enable you to overcome some barriers, such as insufficient funds for a down payment or closing costs, no established credit history, or household expenses higher than the standards traditionally permitted in mortgage lending.

To recap, these mortgage programs include:

- Fannie Mae's and Freddie Mac's Community Lending Programs;
- Subsidized Second Mortgage;
- Community Home Improvement Mortgage Loan; and
- Housing Finance Agency Programs.

Non-conforming or Subprime Loans

If your credit has caused your loan to be denied, you may be considering a non-conforming or subprime loan. A subprime lender charges you a higher interest rate and more points to offset the additional risk you pose because of your credit history. Rates vary a great deal between subprime lenders, so it is important to compare lenders.

In deciding whether you should take a subprime loan, weigh the benefit of paying more interest and points now instead of working to improve your credit and financial management habits.

Many borrowers enter into subprime loans with the intention of refinancing to a cheaper loan once their credit standing improves. If you plan to do this, pay particular attention to whether or not such a loan has a prepayment penalty, which could add costs.

Report Suspected Discrimination

The Equal Credit Opportunity Act and the Fair Housing Act prohibit discrimination against a loan applicant on the basis of race, religion, age, color, national origin, receipt of public assistance funds, sex, or marital status.

If you are a woman, you have a right to your own credit, based on your own credit records and earnings. The lender must count all of your income, including reliable, documented child support and alimony payments (if you choose to disclose these) and part-time employment.

If you suspect that the lender has denied your credit application unfairly, you should report your grievance to the lender's regulatory agency or to the U.S. Department of Housing and Urban Development (HUD), the agency that of enforces the Fair Housing Act.

Summary

This chapter has outlined the steps to help you shop for the most favorable mortgage loan. As we have shown, lenders vary considerably in the rates and terms they offer, so it pays to shop around. You will need a good deal of information to compare various lenders' policies and terms. Approach your information-gathering systematically; be specific about your needs and ask questions. When you find a lender that offers the mortgage and terms you want, request a loan application and schedule a loan interview. Following the application processing, you will be notified whether your application has been accepted. If your application denied, find out why and take steps to correct the situation. If your application is approved, you're well on your way to homeownership. In the next chapter, we look at what is involved in closing—finalizing the loan, issuing the mortgage, and getting the keys to your new house!

CHAPTER 4

Closing

Overview

The mortgage loan closing (or "settlement," as it is called in some parts of the country) is the meeting in which your loan is finalized, your mortgage is issued, and you get the keys to your new house.

In this chapter, we look at what needs to happen in the final weeks before closing, such as the title search, a survey of the property, and your final walk-through inspection. We then run through what you can expect on the closing day, including signing documents and paying closing costs. We also explain the costs that the buyer pays at closing. Although there is no standard settlement process that is followed nationwide, the following description of the process will give you an idea of what to expect.

Preparing for Closing

The final days and weeks prior to closing can be a stressful period for both buyer and seller. For example, you may have second thoughts about taking on such a large debt. Or, you may worry that something will happen to prevent the sale—and indeed the house is not yours until you close on it.

However, the signed sales contract and the signed loan commitment letter obligate both you and the seller to complete the transaction. In fact, if you fail to do so, not only will you forfeit your (earnest money) deposit, but you may also find yourself embroiled in a lawsuit.

Setting the Closing Date

The closing date is set after your loan has been approved and the commitment letter is accepted. Often, the real estate sales professional will coordinate this date with you, the seller, your lender, and the closing agent. You need to be sure that closing takes place before the lender's commitment and the rate lock-in expire. You can now make definite moving plans.

Selecting a Settlement Agent

In different parts of the country, closings are either conducted by lending institutions, title insurance companies, escrow companies, real estate brokers, or attorneys for the buyer or seller. You may have some flexibility and be able to save money by shopping around for a settlement agent. The "Settlement costs worksheet" (Worksheet 10, page 87) is included for this purpose.

Meeting Conditions of the Loan Offer

Be sure you understand the conditions of the loan offer in the lender's commitment letter. If the home is in violation of a building code or zoning regulation, the commitment letter may specify that those problems must be corrected before the closing. If the seller has agreed to make repairs required by the lender, you will want to make sure the work is finished (and done properly) before closing.

Securing Title Services

Before the closing, a title search on the property is required.

Title search...
Lenders require a title search to make sure the borrower will receive clean title to the property. They want to be sure that the seller is indeed the owner of the property. The title search also attempts to uncover any encumbrances on the title. This includes liens (legal claims against a property) filed by creditors in an attempt to collect unpaid bills, as well as liens filed by the IRS for nonpayment of taxes. Any such claims against the property must be paid by the seller before or at closing. The buyer typically pays for the title search.

Title insurance...
As further insurance that the seller is giving the buyer a marketable title, the lender will require title insurance. There are two types of policies:

- A lender's policy; and
- An owner's policy.

The lender's policy protects the lender in the event a flaw in the title is detected after the property has been bought. The owner's policy protects you. Generally you pay the cost of both, and obtaining a combined lender's/owner's policy will save money. You also may get a price break if the company that previously insured the title gives you a reissue policy.

Survey

The lender may require a survey of the property before closing. This is done to confirm that the property's boundaries are as described in the purchase and sale agreement. This is another charge that is normally paid by the buyer. This survey, or plot plan, may show that a neighbor's fence extends onto the seller's property (or vice versa). Sometimes more serious violations are uncovered. Some properties also come with certain easements, which refers to a right to the use of, or access to,

the property. Again, you may be able to save money by requesting an update from a surveyor who has examined the property previously.

Termite Certificate

In many locations, termite inspections are required before a home can be sold. Usually the seller pays for this. The buyer will get a certificate from a termite inspection firm that states that the property is free of both visible termite infestation and termite damage.

Homeowner's Insurance

Your lender will require that you purchase homeowner's or hazard insurance, which protects you and the lender from loss in the event the house is damaged or destroyed by fire or storm. Most homebuyers purchase an insurance package that includes:

- Personal liability insurance, which protects you in the event you are sued by someone who is injured on your property or injured by a member of your family, except in an automobile accident; and
- Coverage against fire, theft, and certain weather-related hazards (various options are available).

You will want to get quotes from several companies describing what types of coverage your homeowner's policy should include and how much coverage you need. Generally the lender will require only minimal coverage up to the replacement value of the house.

When comparing quotes from different companies, be sure they are for the same types and amounts of coverage. In some cases, it may be advantageous to take over the seller's existing insurance policy. In other cases, the lender may recommend a particular policy. Or, use an insurance company with which you already do business; you may save money by having two or more policies (for example, your automobile insurance and your homeowner's insurance). In any case, make sure the coverage is what you want and need.

By requesting a higher deductible amount (the insurance company pays losses only above the deductible amount), you can significantly reduce your insurance costs. That way, you pay for minor damage yourself but have protection against major losses.

Lenders typically want the first year's premium to be paid at or before closing. A lender may insist on adding the subsequent hazard insurance premiums to your monthly mortgage payments to ensure that the policy remains in effect for the life of the loan. The lender will keep this portion of your payments in an escrow account and pay the bill each year. If you are obtaining the insurance on your own, you will need to bring the policy and paid receipt with you to the closing.

Type of Ownership

Are you going to be the sole owner or are you buying the home jointly—either with your spouse or with one or more other partners? The name or names on the deed must normally be the same as those who will be responsible for the mortgage.

In the sales contract, you already may have specified the type of ownership interest. This is something you may wish to discuss with a real estate attorney. The chief options are:

- Sole ownership—you are the only owner;
- Tenancy by the entirety—available only to married couples, both owners have to agree before the house can be sold or even refinanced; when one spouse dies, the house automatically goes to the surviving spouse without going through "probate" (the legal process by which property is distributed after someone's death);
- Joint tenancy—during their lifetimes, any of the owners may sell their interest to whomever they choose; when one owner dies, the surviving owner automatically gets the deceased owner's share in the property; and

- Tenancy in common—the property is owned jointly, but if one owner dies, the deceased owner's share goes to his or her heirs rather than the surviving owner.

Homeowner's Warranty

If you're buying a new house, you should receive a homeowner's warranty protecting against certain defects in your home. Both the homeowner's warranty and a certificate of occupancy should be provided at closing. Without a certificate of occupancy, it's illegal to live in a newly constructed home. Recently, homeowner's warranties have become available for older homes as well, typically covering repair of the major systems during the first year of ownership. If you are considering buying such a policy or accepting a policy provided by the seller, look carefully to see which problems are covered.

Final Walk-through Inspection

Your contract should have included a clause allowing you to examine the property within 24 hours prior to closing. This allows you to make sure that the seller has vacated the house and left behind whatever property (such as appliances) that was agreed upon. You can also make sure that all conditions in the contract have been satisfied. Typically, the real estate sales professional (often both the selling and the listing agents) will accompany you.

If your sales contract made the seller responsible for plumbing, heating, mechanical, and electrical systems in working order at the time of the settlement, this is your last chance to make sure that everything works. During the walk-through, all remaining deficiencies should be noted. If they cannot be corrected before settlement, funds may be withheld from the seller by the settlement attorney for payment of the agreed-upon repairs. If during the walk-through you observe major problems or violations of the purchase contract, you have the right to hold up settlement until they are corrected. A secondary inspection generally is conducted after any repairs are completed and added to the file.

House tour with seller...

It is wise, if at all possible, to make an appointment to tour the house room by room with the seller—you can do this either before or shortly after the closing—and come prepared with questions and a note pad, perhaps even a tape recorder. You'll want to find out the location of the following:

- Main cutoff valves for water and gas;
- Emergency switch on the furnace;
- Hot water heater thermostat;
- Main electrical switch; and
- Fuse or circuit breaker box.

Bring along labels to mark the switches and cutoff valves.

Does the seller know something of the history of the house? Are there old photographs that you might get copied? Are there wiring diagrams or plans for renovations that were never carried out? Who supplies the fuel oil? What day is the garbage picked up? Try to get the names and phone numbers of contractors and other professionals (electricians, plumbers, roofers, carpenters) who have worked on the house and find out what they did and when. What kinds of seasonal maintenance did the seller do? Are there trees that require pruning or plants that require special care? Be sure to find out where the cutoff valve is for any outside faucets. If you're lucky, the seller will remember to tell you that the outside faucet will freeze if you don't drain it before winter.

Final Estimate of Closing Costs

In times past, buyers dreaded closing day because they frequently were hit with hundreds or even thousands of dollars in unexpected closing costs. Today, the situation has changed for the better. You will know in advance exactly what costs you will be responsible for and the approximate amount.

The lender is required to give you an estimate of closing costs soon after you have filed your application for a loan (see Chapter 3). Since these estimates are subject to change, you have the right to

inspect the settlement form (called the HUD–1 Settlement Statement) one business day before settlement. It is useful to do so because you probably will be required to pay the remainder of the down payment (minus the amount of your earnest money deposit) and closing costs with a certified or cashier's check. A personal check may not be acceptable.

If You Need Help with Closing Costs

For many prospective homebuyers, coming up with closing or settlement costs can be difficult. For this reason, it's important to consider your settlement fees before you make your purchase offer. As we noted in Chapter 3, it also pays to shop for competitive pricing for as many services as possible and to negotiate with the seller over who will pay what costs.

Closing—the Big Day!

In most places, the closing is a formal meeting typically attended by the buyer, seller, listing and selling agents, and representatives of the lender and title company. (In some areas there is no formal closing in which the buyer and seller and the real estate sales professionals sit down with the closing agent. Instead an escrow agent processes all the paperwork and collects and disburses the required funds.) You may consider hiring a real estate attorney to attend your closing, advise you concerning the signing of papers, and represent your interests at this final important meeting. You will be asked to sign numerous documents and affidavits, you will pay the closing costs assigned to you, and you will be given the keys to your new house!

Let's look a little closer at what you can expect at closing.

The Closing Documents

A significant part of the process of closing is the explanation and signing of various documents. These are described here.

HUD-1 Settlement Statement...

This form, required by federal law, itemizes the services provided and lists the charges to the buyer and seller. It is filled out by the settlement agent who conducts the closing. Both the buyer and seller must sign it.

Truth-in-lending (TIL) statement...

This is another document required by federal law that mortgage lenders must give to all loan applicants within three business days of receiving their initial application. Among other things, it discloses the annual percentage rate (APR), which reflects the cost of your mortgage as a yearly rate. This rate may be higher than the interest rate stated in your mortgage because the APR includes any points, fees, and other costs of credit. The TIL statement also sets forth the other terms of the loan, including the finance charge, amount financed, and total payments required.

Should the actual APR differ by more than a small amount from the lender's original estimate, the lender must give you a corrected TIL statement no later than at settlement. The lender does not need to give you a new TIL statement if the estimated APR proves correct, even if other disclosures have changed. For this reason, it's a good idea to check with the lender shortly before closing to see whether all the TIL disclosures are still accurate.

The note...

The mortgage note represents your promise to pay the lender according to the agreed terms. It is, in effect, a legal "IOU." Again, the terms of the loan are set forth, including the date on which your payments must be made and the location to which they must be sent.

The note also details the penalties that will be assessed if you default (that is, if you fall behind in paying the loan) and warns you that the lender can "call" the loan (require full repayment before the end of the loan term) if you fail to make the required payments, if you sell the house without prior written consent of the lender, or if you otherwise violate the terms of your note or mortgage.

The mortgage...

The mortgage (or deed of trust in some localities) is the legal document that secures the note and gives the lender a claim against your house if you default on the note's terms. In effect, you have possession of the property, but the lender has partial ownership (called an "encumbrance") until the loan has been fully repaid.

The mortgage restates the basic information contained in the note as well as the date of the final scheduled payment. It states the responsibilities of the borrower to pay principal and interest, taxes, and insurance in a timely manner; to maintain hazard insurance on the property without lapse; and to maintain the property.

The mortgage also states that if the borrower fails to comply with these requirements, the lender can demand full payment of the loan balance. Moreover, if the borrower defaults, the lender can foreclose on the property, sell it, and use the proceeds to pay off the outstanding loan, accrued interest, and the foreclosure costs. The borrower will receive anything left over after any liens (legal claims against a property) and second or third mortgages are repaid.

In some states, a deed of trust is used instead of a mortgage. Under a deed of trust, the buyer/borrower receives title to the property but conveys title to a third-party trustee by signing a deed of trust. You keep the original recorded deed from the seller. The trustee holds title until the entire loan balance is paid.

Affidavits...

You may be asked to sign numerous affidavits (for example, that it is your intention to occupy the property). These may be required by state law, by the lender, or by the secondary market agencies. If you provide false information, you can face criminal penalties and run the risk of the lender calling your loan.

The deed...

The seller must bring the deed to the closing, properly signed and notarized. It is the document

A. **Settlement Statement**

U.S. Department of Housing
and Urban Development

OMB Approval No. 2502-0265
(expires 9/30/2006)

B. Type of Loan

1. ☐ FHA	2. ☐ FmHA	3. ☐ Conv. Unins.	6. File Number:	7. Loan Number:	8. Mortgage Insurance Case Number:
4. ☐ VA	5. ☐ Conv. Ins.				

C. Note: This form is furnished to give you a statement of actual settlement costs. Amounts paid to and by the settlement agent are shown. Items marked "(p.o.c.)" were paid outside the closing; they are shown here for informational purposes and are not included in the totals.

D. Name & Address of Borrower:	E. Name & Address of Seller:	F. Name & Address of Lender:

G. Property Location:	H. Settlement Agent:	
	Place of Settlement:	I. Settlement Date:

J. Summary of Borrower's Transaction		**K. Summary of Seller's Transaction**	
100. Gross Amount Due From Borrower		**400. Gross Amount Due To Seller**	
101. Contract sales price		401. Contract sales price	
102. Personal property		402. Personal property	
103. Settlement charges to borrower (line 1400)		403.	
104.		404.	
105.		405.	
Adjustments for items paid by seller in advance		**Adjustments for items paid by seller in advance**	
106. City/town taxes to		406. City/town taxes to	
107. County taxes to		407. County taxes to	
108. Assessments to		408. Assessments to	
109.		409.	
110.		410.	
111.		411.	
112.		412.	
120. Gross Amount Due From Borrower		**420. Gross Amount Due To Seller**	
200. Amounts Paid By Or In Behalf Of Borrower		**500. Reductions In Amount Due To Seller**	
201. Deposit or earnest money		501. Excess deposit (see instructions)	
202. Principal amount of new loan(s)		502. Settlement charges to seller (line 1400)	
203. Existing loan(s) taken subject to		503. Existing loan(s) taken subject to	
204.		504. Payoff of first mortgage loan	
205.		505. Payoff of second mortgage loan	
206.		506.	
207.		507.	
208.		508.	
209.		509.	
Adjustments for items unpaid by seller		**Adjustments for items unpaid by seller**	
210. City/town taxes to		510. City/town taxes to	
211. County taxes to		511. County taxes to	
212. Assessments to		512. Assessments to	
213.		513.	
214.		514.	
215.		515.	
216.		516.	
217.		517.	
218.		518.	
219.		519.	
220. Total Paid By/For Borrower		**520. Total Reduction Amount Due Seller**	
300. Cash At Settlement From/To Borrower		**600. Cash At Settlement To/From Seller**	
301. Gross Amount due from borrower (line 120)		601. Gross amount due to seller (line 420)	
302. Less amounts paid by/for borrower (line 220)	( )	602. Less reductions in amt. due seller (line 520)	( )
303. Cash ☐ From ☐ To Borrower		**603. Cash** ☐ To ☐ From Seller	

Section 5 of the Real Estate Settlement Procedures Act (RESPA) requires the following: • HUD must develop a Special Information Booklet to help persons borrowing money to finance the purchase of residential real estate to better understand the nature and costs of real estate settlement services; • Each lender must provide the booklet to all applicants from whom it receives or for whom it prepares a written application to borrow money to finance the purchase of residential real estate; • Lenders must prepare and distribute with the Booklet a Good Faith Estimate of the settlement costs that the borrower is likely to incur in connection with the settlement. These disclosures are manadatory.

Section 4(a) of RESPA mandates that HUD develop and prescribe this standard form to be used at the time of loan settlement to provide full disclosure of all charges imposed upon the borrower and seller. These are third party disclosures that are designed to provide the borrower with pertinent information during the settlement process in order to be a better shopper.

The Public Reporting Burden for this collection of information is estimated to average one hour per response, including the time for reviewing instructions, searching existing data sources, gathering and maintaining the data needed, and completing and reviewing the collection of information.

This agency may not collect this information, and you are not required to complete this form, unless it displays a currently valid OMB control number.

The information requested does not lend itself to confidentiality.

Previous editions are obsolete

Page 1 of 2

form **HUD-1** (3/86)
ref Handbook 4305.2

L. Settlement Charges

			Paid From Borrowers Funds at Settlement	Paid From Seller's Funds at Settlement
700. Total Sales/Broker's Commission based on price $ @ % =				
Division of Commission (line 700) as follows:				
701. $	to			
702. $	to			
703. Commission paid at Settlement				
704.				
800. Items Payable In Connection With Loan				
801. Loan Origination Fee	%			
802. Loan Discount	%			
803. Appraisal Fee	to			
804. Credit Report	to			
805. Lender's Inspection Fee				
806. Mortgage Insurance Application Fee to				
807. Assumption Fee				
808.				
809.				
810.				
811.				
900. Items Required By Lender To Be Paid In Advance				
901. Interest from to @$ /day				
902. Mortgage Insurance Premium for months to				
903. Hazard Insurance Premium for years to				
904. years to				
905.				
1000. Reserves Deposited With Lender				
1001. Hazard insurance	months@$	per month		
1002. Mortgage insurance	months@$	per month		
1003. City property taxes	months@$	per month		
1004. County property taxes	months@$	per month		
1005. Annual assessments	months@$	per month		
1006.	months@$	per month		
1007.	months@$	per month		
1008.	months@$	per month		
1100. Title Charges				
1101. Settlement or closing fee	to			
1102. Abstract or title search	to			
1103. Title examination	to			
1104. Title insurance binder	to			
1105. Document preparation	to			
1106. Notary fees	to			
1107. Attorney's fees	to			
(includes above items numbers:)				
1108. Title insurance	to			
(includes above items numbers:)				
1109. Lender's coverage	$			
1110. Owner's coverage	$			
1111.				
1112.				
1113.				
1200. Government Recording and Transfer Charges				
1201. Recording fees: Deed $; Mortgage $; Releases $				
1202. City/county tax/stamps: Deed $; Mortgage $				
1203. State tax/stamps: Deed $; Mortgage $				
1204.				
1205.				
1300. Additional Settlement Charges				
1301. Survey to				
1302. Pest inspection to				
1303.				
1304.				
1305.				
1400. Total Settlement Charges (enter on lines 103, Section J and 502, Section K)				

that transfers ownership from the seller to you. As discussed previously, you should have decided what name or names are to appear on the deed.

Allocation of closing costs...
We will now briefly discuss the various costs that are likely to be paid by the seller. Note, however, that local custom varies and, in addition, who pays the various closing costs can be negotiated between the buyer and seller (and should be specified in the sales contract). While it is possible to have an agreement in which the buyer OR the seller pays all closing costs, typically these costs are shared by both.

Fees paid to the lender...
Certain fees are typically paid to the lender at closing.

Loan origination fee. This fee covers the administrative costs of processing the loan. It may be expressed as a percentage of the loan (for example, 1 percent of the mortgage amount).

Loan discount points. These are the points charged by a lender to adjust the yield on the loan to market conditions. Each point equals 1 percent of the mortgage amount.

Appraisal fee. This pays for the appraisal, which the lender uses to determine whether the value of the property is sufficient to secure the loan should you default on the loan. The fee is usually paid by you when you apply for the mortgage and may show on the settlement sheet as "POC," or "paid outside closing."

Credit report fee. This covers the cost of the credit report, which the lender used to determine your creditworthiness. Like the appraisal fee, you probably paid this fee when you applied for the mortgage.

Assumption fee. You pay this processing fee if you take over the payments on the seller's existing loan.

Advance payments or prepays...
The lender may require you to prepay some or all of the following items at the time of settlement.

Interest. You will probably have to pay the interest on the mortgage from the date of settlement to the beginning of the period covered by the first monthly payment. For example, suppose you settle on February 10. Your first monthly payment begins to accrue on March 1 and will be payable at the beginning of April. At closing you may be required to prepay the interest for the period from February 10 through the end of February. This means that if you settle later in the month, your closing costs will be less than if you settle early in the month.

Mortgage insurance premium. The lender may require you to pay your first year's premium or a lump sum premium at settlement. (As noted earlier, ask your lender about programs that do not require a lump sum payment at closing.)

Hazard insurance premium. You may be required to pay the first year's premium at settlement. Or, you may need to bring proof that you already have paid for the policy.

Escrow accounts or reserves...
Reserves are required if the lender will be paying your property taxes, mortgage insurance, and hazard insurance. Again, state and local law and lenders' policies vary.

Title charges...
These primarily are charges payable to companies or persons other than the lender. This includes the settlement (or closing) fee, title search/title insurance premium (lender's and owner's coverage), document preparation fees, and attorney fees (for legal services provided to the lender). Note that the fees you pay for your own real estate attorney are not part of the settlement procedures.

Recording and transfer fees...
Most states impose a tax on the transfer of property and require payment of a fee for recording the purchase documents.

Additional charges...
Included here are the surveyor's fees, charges for termite and other pest infestation inspections, and any other inspections required by the lender.

Adjustments...

Another part of the settlement costing-out involves looking at items paid by the seller in advance and items yet to be paid for which the seller is responsible. The most common expense to be prorated between the buyer and seller is property taxes, which are split so that you take responsibility for them beginning at settlement. If the seller already has paid taxes beyond that date, you reimburse the seller; if taxes for the current period have not yet been paid, the amount owed is deducted from the buyer's settlement payment.

Final reckoning—the bottom line...

In calculating the total amount that the borrower must pay, the settlement statement begins with the sales price and adds in the total closing costs for which you are responsible. Any prorated adjustments payable by you (as discussed above) are then added in.

Your earnest money deposit, which has been held in escrow since the seller signed your purchase offer, and the principal amount of your mortgage or of any existing loan being assumed is deducted from the total. Then, any adjustments payable by the seller are deducted. The resulting figure is the amount you owe at settlement.

Recording the documents...

After all the papers have been signed and the fees have been paid, the mortgage or deed of trust, and the deed must officially be recorded, usually at the registry of deeds or the town clerk's office. The closing agent usually will not release the checks to the seller or the agent until the transaction has been recorded, making the buyer the official owner of record. This legal transfer of the property usually takes place one to two days after settlement.

The Keys to Your New Home!

Real estate sales professionals say that the house keys are the one item that sellers most commonly forget to bring to settlement. You will want to make sure you get the keys for all the doors (basement, garage, etc.) and then have the locks changed.

Summary

This chapter has outlined the basic process of closing or settlement on your home purchase. Closing need not be a stressful experience if you know what to expect and prepare for it. Preparing for closing involves some basic steps: setting the closing date; selecting a settlement agent; meeting the conditions (if any) of the loan commitment; securing title services, a survey of the property, a termite certificate, homeowner's insurance, and a homeowner's warranty (if you desire it); and making a final walk-through inspection on the day before closing. The actual closing meeting itself involves the explanation and signing of the closing documents, the allocation and payment of closing costs, and getting the keys. At this point, your obligations as a homeowner—repaying the loan and maintaining your property—have begun. In the final chapter, we look at some of the joys and responsibilities you will face.

CHAPTER 5

Life as a Homeowner

Overview

Congratulations on becoming a homeowner! Before the excitement of being a new homeowner fades, read this chapter. Your responsibilities as a homeowner—including repaying the loan and maintaining the property—have just begun. This final chapter discusses the steps you need to take to protect your investment, particularly paying your mortgage on time each month. We also look at the steps you can take to avoid foreclosure and the loss of your home—including living within a household budget and saving ahead for unexpected problems. We conclude by looking at the financial benefits of homeownership, including the potential for substantial tax breaks and how to take advantage of home equity without selling your house.

Settling in

Now that you have successfully made your way through the home-buying process, no doubt you're anxious to move into your new house. Depending on how much you have to move and how far you are moving, this can be a do-it-yourself job or one to leave to professionals. In either case, this is a good time to go through your belongings and get rid of anything you don't need or want. This will make the packing easier and cut down on what you need to find room for in your new home.

Meet the Neighbors

Make it a point to introduce yourself and your family to your neighbors as soon as possible. They can be an invaluable source of information, especially when you're new to a community. Knowing your neighbors and getting involved in community affairs is both personally rewarding and a way of protecting your home.

Homeowner & Neighborhood Associations

As soon as possible, find out about homeowner or neighborhood associations. Some condominium associations or other neighborhoods may require owners to become members. It's a good idea to get a copy of the rules and regulations before moving in.

Safety Tips

Once you've moved in, be sure to take these simple safety steps.

Emergency numbers...
Find the location and jot down the phone numbers of the nearest hospital, local police precinct, and fire station. Does "911" serve as an all-purpose emergency number in your area?

Theft prevention...
The day you move in (if not before), change all the door locks to deadbolts and get new keys. You have no way of knowing how many sets of keys there might be to the existing locks and who has them. Lock your windows and doors when you are not at home. Always alert a neighbor if you're going to be away for more than a few days.

Fire safety...

You can prevent possible disaster by eliminating fire hazards and installing smoke detectors and fire extinguishers.

Smoke detectors. Make sure that smoke detectors are installed outside each bedroom door, in or near the living room, and on each floor. Check them at least twice a year (for example, each spring and fall when you readjust your clocks for daylight savings time) to ensure they are still in working order.

Fire extinguishers. Buy at least two fire extinguishers and hang them so they are easily accessible from the kitchen and from the main living area. For a larger house, place additional extinguishers in the garage, the basement, and on each floor.

Fire-prevention inspection tour. Many communities will send a fire inspector to your home upon request to help you identify fire hazards, such as frayed electrical cords, an overloaded electrical system, and clutter in the basement or attic. If this service is not available, do your own inspection tour.

Evacuation plan. Develop with your family a plan for leaving your home in case of a fire. Make sure that each member of your family, including your children, knows the closest and safest exits depending on the location of the fire. Your evacuation plan should include where your family will meet outside. For example, you might decide that all family members will meet at the sidewalk in front of the house or in your next door neighbor's front yard.

Carbon monoxide detectors...

Carbon monoxide (CO) is a colorless, odorless, and deadly gas. Because you can't see, taste, or smell it, CO can kill before anyone knows it's there. Today's more energy-efficient, airtight home designs can trap CO-polluted air inside. The U.S. Consumer Product Safety Commission recommends installing at least one carbon monoxide detector per household near the sleeping area. A second detector near the home's heating source adds an extra measure of safety.

Storing valuables...

Collect your important papers (don't forget the deed to your house and your mortgage documents) and store them in a safe place, such as a fireproof box or a safe deposit box.

Insurance coverage...

Insurance coverage is an essential part of protecting your home; make sure it is complete and up-to-date. Review your existing insurance plans with your insurance agent to eliminate coverage duplication and find opportunities for savings.

Homeowner's insurance. You already will have bought homeowner's insurance, as well as flood insurance if you are in a federally designated flood area. These are required by lenders before closing (see Chapter 4). Your homeowner's insurance policy may include an inflation rider, which automatically increases the coverage as the value of the property increases. If not, check each time you renew the policy to ensure that the replacement value specified by the insurance keeps up with the current market value of your house. Otherwise, you risk not being reimbursed for the full amount of the damage. Standard coverage normally insures personal belongings at 50 percent to 70 percent of the value of the dwelling. Individuals may want to consider increasing their coverage to a higher percentage—say, 75 percent—in light of the actual costs they will face to replace their possessions. Also, see how much coverage is provided for special items, such as computer equipment, jewelry, silverware, or a valuable coin or stamp collection. You may decide to purchase additional coverage for these items.

Home warranties. Home warranties reimburse homeowners for repair costs not covered by their homeowner's insurance policy. Generally, a warranty will cover breakdowns of major appliances such as washers, driers, ovens, and refrigerators as well as plumbing, electrical, heating, and air-conditioning systems. If you purchased a new home, the builder probably supplied a home warranty policy. In some instances, a seller may purchase a warranty to increase the marketability of his/her home. Homeowners also may purchase this coverage themselves.

Because this type of insurance is not regulated, the owner must understand what the policy covers. Also, a home warranty is only as secure as the company that offers it; investigate the reliability of the company carefully before making a commitment.

Mortgage life insurance. This type of insurance pays off the mortgage in the event of the borrower's death. Make sure that your existing life insurance doesn't already provide such coverage before purchasing this separate policy. Also be sure to tailor your insurance to your own circumstances. For example, a single homeowner with no dependents might decide that mortgage life insurance is unnecessary. Your insurance agent can assist you in matching your needs with available options.

Getting to Know Your New Home

As a new homeowner, there are many things you may previously have taken for granted. Learn enough about the major systems of the house to perform routine maintenance and handle various emergencies. Each adult member of the household should know the location of the following:

- Main cutoff valves for water and gas;
- Emergency switch for the furnace or burner;
- Hot water heater thermostat;
- Main electrical switch; and
- Fuse or circuit breaker box.

House file...
It is a good idea to set up a house file that includes warranties, owner's manuals, and other documents from the previous owner. Add to it repair, routine maintenance, and improvement records you undertake.

Meeting Your Obligations as a Borrower

As a new homeowner, the importance of making your mortgage payment on time each month cannot be overemphasized. The purchase of a home may be the biggest investment you'll ever make and you certainly don't want to jeopardize it. Making late payments can result in late charges and will

damage your credit rating. Failing to make payments can result in even more serious consequences—it will set in motion the lender's action to foreclose, evict you, and sell your home. You can prevent this by consistently making your payments on time. But if you cannot keep up with your payments, discuss your situation with your lender immediately.

Understanding the Terms of Your Loan

At the closing or settlement, you signed both the note (a legal "IOU" to the lender) and the mortgage (or deed of trust), the legal document that secures the note and gives the lender a legal claim against your property if you default on the note's terms. (See Chapter 4 for more information.) If you feel overwhelmed, remember that the lender has confidence in your ability to repay the mortgage or you wouldn't have been approved for the loan in the first place.

Payment terms...
Make sure you know when your payments are due (normally the first day of the month) and where to send them. The lender will provide you with a payment book to help you keep track of your payments or will send you monthly billing statements. If you have received neither, contact your lender. Don't wait until a mortgage payment is overdue.

You may be charged a late fee if your payment is received after the grace period specified in your mortgage note, usually the 15th of the month. (Remember, the lender must RECEIVE the payment by the date indicated on your mortgage note. Placing the check in the mailbox on the date due will NOT satisfy this requirement.) Sending in late payments will give you a bad payment record and could be a mark against you if you need an extension on a payment. Ask your lender about having your mortgage payment automatically drafted from your checking account if you foresee problems in mailing your payments on time.

ARM terms...
If you have an adjustable-rate mortgage (ARM), your payments may change over time. Refer to your legal documents to find out how frequently

payment and interest rate changes may occur and under what circumstances. If you have any questions, contact your lender immediately and ask them to explain the calculation.

Other terms...

When you want to sell your house or refinance your mortgage loan, can you pay off your loan without a prepayment penalty? Can the buyer assume, or take over, your mortgage? Your mortgage documents should provide the answers to these questions. If you're uncertain, don't hesitate to contact your lender.

Transfer of Servicing

Many lenders transfer the responsibility of collecting and processing your mortgage payments to another lender or servicer after your loan is closed. In fact, at the closing or settlement, one of the documents you should receive from your lender indicates how frequently they transfer servicing on mortgages they originate.

If your lender transfers your mortgage servicing, the terms will remain unchanged. After the transfer, there is a 60-day grace period. During this time, you cannot be charged a late fee if you send your mortgage payment to the old mortgage servicer. If this happens during the grace period, your new mortgage servicer may not report a late payment to the credit bureau.

Note: Never forward your mortgage payment to a third party unless your current servicer officially notifies of a transfer. If in doubt, contact your servicer to confirm the transfer.

Servicing problems...

If you believe that you have been improperly charged a penalty or late fee, or there are other problems with the servicing of your loan, contact your servicer in writing. The letter should include your account number and explain why your account is incorrect.

Within 20 business days of receiving a written inquiry, the servicer must send you a written response acknowledging the inquiry. Within 60 business days, the servicer must either correct the account or determine that it is accurate. The servicer must send you a written explanation of the action taken.

Escrow adjustments...

If your monthly mortgage payment includes an escrow for homeowner's insurance and property taxes, this portion of your payment may change if the insurance or tax payments change. For example, property tax rates in a community may increase and you may face a larger property tax bill. The servicer will calculate the increase in the monthly escrow and inform you of the payment adjustment. Annual escrow statements. You will receive annual escrow statements from your servicer. Check these updates to make sure that the calculations are correct. If you do not understand an item on the analysis, contact the servicer immediately. Never be embarrassed to get answers to all of your questions!

Cancellation of mortgage insurance...

If you have a conventional loan (that is, a loan that is not an FHA or VA loan) and made less than a 20 percent down payment, you are probably paying private mortgage insurance (PMI). (Remember, private mortgage insurance reimburses lenders and/or investors for some portion of the losses they will face in case of a default.)

Under the Homeowners Protection Act of 1998, for some mortgages closed on and after July 29, 1999, borrowers with a good payment record who have paid off 20 percent of the original mortgage balance—in other words, borrowers with 20 percent equity in their property—may request that their PMI be cancelled. For some mortgages, PMI must be *automatically cancelled* on the date the borrower's equity is scheduled to increase to 22 percent.

On an annual basis, the servicer will disclose important information about PMI cancellation.

If you have an FHA loan, you also may be able to cancel your mortgage insurance. For FHA loans this insurance is known as Mortgage

Insurance Premium (MIP). The process is slightly different. For loans made after January 1, 2001; the MIP automatically will be canceled once the unpaid principal balance, excluding the up-front MIP, reaches 78 percent of the lower of the initial sales price or appraised value.

Homeownership Association Dues

If your new home is part of a homeownership or condominium association, you are responsible for the timely payment of dues. The association has a vested interest in maintaining your property and can initiate legal proceedings if you don't make your payments.

Avoiding Foreclosure

Now that you are a homeowner, your most important financial obligation is your monthly mortgage payment. If you fall behind on your monthly mortgage payments, the lender has the legal right to foreclose on the loan. In the event of foreclosure, the lender can force you to move out and then sell your home to pay off the loan. You risk losing your home, whatever money you have invested in it (including the down payment, closing costs, and all the monthly payments you have made), and your good credit rating. Legal fees also may be added to what you owe if a lender initiates foreclosure proceedings. Even worse, if your property has dropped in value since you bought it, the foreclosure sale may not bring a high enough price to cover your outstanding balance. If this occurs, the lender in some states may have the right to obtain a deficiency judgment and require you to repay the remaining outstanding balance.

If you start having difficulties making your monthly mortgage payments, *you have a serious problem!* Even one missed payment can be difficult to make up. If you find yourself in this situation, you need to get help right away. First, get in touch with your lender (or loan servicer) *immediately* to explain your situation. Also consider all possible resources. Is there a relative you might be able to borrow from? Do you have a profit-sharing plan or an insurance policy you can

borrow from? Can you cut back, at least temporarily, on other expenses? Can you work overtime or get a second, part-time job? Look for a local accredited credit counseling agency to help you organize your finances and establish a workable repayment plan.

Note: Don't be tempted to catch up on missed mortgage payments by taking out a short-term loan from a loan company or by taking a cash advance on your credit card. The interest rate on consumer credit is very high and may result in more serious financial trouble later.

Contacting your lender (or servicer)...
When they encounter financial problems, some people avoid calling their creditors for as long as possible. This is the wrong strategy if you wish to keep your home. If you put off doing anything in hopes that your financial situation will improve, you risk losing your home!

When you call the lender (or the servicer to whom you send your monthly payments), explain that your payments are overdue and explain why you have been unable to make them. For example, you were laid off from your job or you have been sick and are temporarily unable to work. Get the name of the person you talk with and write a follow-up letter for your loan file. If you can't reach your lender by phone, put this same information in a letter and ask the lender to contact you. In either case, your letter to the lender should include the following information:

- Your name;
- Loan number;
- Property address;
- Your daytime and evening telephone numbers; and
- Brief explanation of why you are unable to make the mortgage payment.

Your lender (or servicer) will be willing to work with you, provided the lender believes you are acting in good faith (that is, you sincerely want to make your monthly mortgage payments and keep your home). Again, the lender will be more likely to consider repayment options if you have had a good payment history and you initiate contact at the outset.

Working with a housing counselor...

If the lender thinks there is a reasonable chance that you can bring the mortgage current, the lender may refer you to a HUD-approved housing counseling agency in your community. A specially trained counselor will work with you to review your budget and establish a workable repayment plan that will enable you to bring your mortgage current.

Some lenders have their own internal counseling programs, however the NFCC recommends that you contact an NFCC HUD-approved housing counseling agency at (866) 845-2227.

Depending on your circumstances, the lender may offer you temporary or permanent assistance. For example, the lender might agree to reduce or suspend your monthly payments for a specified period, after which you would resume your regular payments and pay an additional amount each month to make up for the delinquency. In extreme cases, the lender may even be willing to change the terms of your mortgage (for example, by lowering the interest rate, converting an adjustable-rate mortgage to a fixed rate, or extending the repayment term) in order to reduce your monthly payments.

If your lender does not refer you to a credit counselor and you are unable to reach a workable agreement, contact a local housing counseling agency. Some of these agencies offer free help to homeowners having trouble keeping up with their mortgage payments.

Beware of unscrupulous "buyers"...

Unscrupulous individuals and firms sometimes try to take advantage of homeowners facing financial difficulties. Many homeowners have been victimized by "buyers" making false claims. One such "distressed homeowner" program targets those who can't make their monthly payments but are in a negative equity position (that is, their mortgage is more than the sales value of their property). The homeowner pays the "buyer" a fee and transfers title to the house, which is subsequently sold.

Firms offering such programs falsely claim that by transferring the property to a third party, homeowners can walk away from their obligations without getting a bad credit record. If you decide that the only way out of your financial difficulty is to sell the house, get advice from your lender, your credit counselor, or a real estate attorney before signing any kind of sales agreement.

Maintaining Your Home

Now that you're a homeowner, you can't afford to sit back and wait for something to break before you fix it. In many cases, you can extend the life of major systems and avoid expensive repairs by doing preventive maintenance. You also need to take care of your yard. This may entail cleaning up around the trash receptacles, mowing the lawn, watering plants, raking leaves, and shoveling sidewalks. Proper maintenance of your home also will help protect your investment.

Seasonal Inspection Checklist

Put together a seasonal checklist and mark your calendar so you'll remember to use it. Once you get the routine down it will be well worth the trouble. See Worksheet 11 (page 89), "Seasonal home maintenance schedule," to get you started. The checklist should reflect your own home's systems and needs.

Cost-effective Energy Conservation Measures

It comes as a shock to many first-time homeowners to discover the high cost of utilities. After the heating and/or air conditioning bills start coming in, you may be eager to evaluate where you can start to conserve energy. There are many low-cost ways to improve the energy efficiency of a home that don't require specialized skills. You might check the following areas:

- Do you need more insulation?
- Are there storm windows all around?
- Is weather stripping and caulking needed?
- Is the attic properly ventilated?
- Is the room temperature controlled by a timed (programmable) thermostat?

Contact your local utility or state agency for energy-saving tips specific to your geographic area. Also find out about federal tax rebates and utility company incentives for installing energy-efficient heating and cooling systems. Again, this is not a one-time effort. Your spring and fall inspection tours should include home maintenance procedures aimed at cutting your energy bills.

Finally, you can always contact your local weatherization program. Some low-income families might be eligible for free energy efficiency repairs, including new furnaces, water heaters, and insulation.

Do-it-yourself Repairs

You won't need expensive tools or much experience to do many basic home repairs yourself. Making small repairs before they become big projects can save you both money and aggravation. You may want to take a home repair course at a local community college, hardware store, or building supplier. Or borrow a basic home maintenance book or video from your public library. You'll be pleased to discover that you don't need to hire a carpenter to replace a broken windowpane or a plumber to fix a leaky faucet. You can do a lot with just a few basic tools:

- Hammer;
- Flat-blade and Phillips screwdriver (or a combination screwdriver with interchangeable tips);
- Slip-joint pliers;
- Handsaw;
- Wall scraper;
- Tape measure;
- Flashlight; and
- Plunger.

Major Repairs/Home Improvements

The do-it-yourself approach is good as far as it goes, but sooner or later you'll need to hire an expert. Perhaps you are ready for that new kitchen or bathroom you promised yourself when you moved in. A note of caution. You may want to consider postponing any major renovations for at least a year after you move in to make sure that you are financially able to handle your mortgage payments and routine maintenance expenses. You don't want to incur major expenses right away.

Hiring a contractor…
The following guidelines can help you get such a project done right for a fair price.

- Interview several contractors. Find one that listens to you and with whom you feel comfortable working. Be suspicious of contractors who come to your door to sell their services.
- Get references and check them. Ask friends and neighbors to recommend companies or individuals. Many counties and cities have a licensing process for home improvement contractors. Find out whether the contractor is bonded and carries workmen's compensation insurance for himself and his or her employees. Check with your state's homebuilder's association or contractor association to see if the contractor is a member.
- Get cost estimates and find out whether these are estimates or a firm bid. Often especially with older houses, contractors will not give a firm bid because it's impossible to know until they start the work what they'll find and how hard it will be to fix.
- To protect yourself, especially for a larger job, draw up a contract specifying what work is to be performed and when payments are due. Always hold back part of the payment until after the job is finished.
- Does the job require building permits? If so, who is responsible for obtaining them? Will the work need to be inspected?

Financing major repairs and home improvements...

If you need to make extensive emergency repairs, look for a state or local government program or a nonprofit agency in your area that will help you pay for these repairs. See whether the item needing repair (for example, the heating system or washing machine) is covered by a warranty. Check your homeowner's insurance policy (or call your insurance agent); some repairs (such as water damage) may be covered.

You may be able to obtain a home improvement or a personal loan from a commercial bank or credit union. Sometimes contractors will provide financing for a major project. Or, consider getting a home equity loan (these are discussed later in this chapter). In any case, be sure you understand the terms of the loan and how it is to be repaid. Be sure to shop around for the lowest interest rate. Find out whether monthly payments are required or whether the loan is repayable in one lump sum. And, as noted above, consider postponing unnecessary major renovations until you have lived in your new home at least a year.

Household Budgeting

As a new homeowner, there are undoubtedly lots of things you are anxious to buy—perhaps a lawnmower, a refrigerator, or some new furniture. But wait! Think like a homeowner. Think carefully before you make big purchases, especially if it involves taking on more debt. We already have emphasized that your mortgage payments should be your top financial priority. But you also can't afford to get behind on your utility bills or you risk having your water, electricity, or gas turned off. And if you don't make your car payments, your car may be repossessed. Given the number of credit offers you receive as a new homeowner, it is easy to get overextended quickly. This leads us to the important subject of prioritizing expenses and household budgeting.

Creating a Budget

Most people would like to save more but find it difficult to change their spending patterns. Creating a household budget is the first step to managing your finances. A budget provides a simple method of comparing your income to your expenses on a monthly basis. The process of creating a budget will help you and your family set your goals, establish your priorities, track your spending and identify unwise spending patterns before they lead to financial disaster. You already did much of the work when you calculated your monthly income and expenses in Chapter 1 (see Worksheets 1-4).

To make a monthly budget for your household, complete Worksheet 12 (page 91) following these steps:

Step one: Determine your family's total net income...

You first need to know how much you have to spend each month. For budget purposes, you need to determine your family's total take-home or net pay (income after taxes and other deductions).

If you are paid weekly, multiply your take-home pay by 52 and divide by 12 to get your monthly income. If you are paid every other week, multiply your take-home pay by 26 and divide by 12. Do not include annual bonuses, gifts, income tax refunds, occasional overtime, or other occasional sources of income.

Step two: Determine your total monthly expenses...

You can start with the expense figures you wrote down in Worksheet 1. Be sure to break down your annual, semiannual, and quarterly expenses into monthly figures that can be set aside and will be available when these bills become due. For example, if your car insurance costs $150 every six months, you need to set aside $25 each month to meet this expense.

$150 x 2 = $300 in car insurance payments per year $300 / 12 = $25 set aside per month

Budget tip. Working with a calendar showing each month of the year, "map out" the timing of your monthly expenses (your mortgage, utilities, and car payments) as well as large, periodic expenses, such as property taxes, homeowner's insurance, and car insurance. Make sure that you have set aside enough to cover these periodic expenses and are not caught unaware.

Housing expenses. Be sure to update the housing expenses you calculated in Worksheet 1 to include your actual mortgage payments (and property taxes and homeowner's insurance if you, rather than the lender, pay these directly). Also include your average monthly utility costs (gas, electricity, water and sewage, trash collection, and telephone) and homeowner's association or condo fees, if applicable.

Budget tip: Sign up for your gas and electric companies' "budget" or "average payment" plan. Based on the past history of gas or electric use in your home, the company arrives at an estimated annual cost, then divides it by 12 months. Regardless of your actual consumption, you are billed the same amount every month. Once a year, the company will adjust your monthly payment up or down to reflect your actual use, after which you continue to pay the new amount for another year. Paying a set amount each month helps tremendously with budgeting since it spreads the high cost of winter heating, for example, throughout the year.

Home maintenance allowance. Now that you are a homeowner, you need to budget for regular home maintenance and emergency repairs. Some financial advisors suggest allocating 1 percent of the purchase price of the house for annual maintenance and repairs. For example,

Purchase Price of your home: $80,000 x 1 percent x .01 annual allowance to pay for home maintenance and repairs = $800

To calculate how much to set aside each month, $800 / 12 months = $65.

So, each month, in this example, you would plan to set aside $65 for home maintenance expenses. Of

course, the amount you budget should reflect your own situation. Your maintenance costs may be considerably higher if you have an older house with the original plumbing, wiring, furnace, and roof.

Non-housing expenses. Now look at the non-housing expenses you listed in Worksheet 1. For budget purposes, don't include any expenses (such as income taxes and health insurance) that are already deducted from your paycheck. Do include the debt payments you itemized in Worksheet 4.

Budget tip: How much debt is too much? You can easily calculate your debt-to-net income ratio by dividing your total monthly debt payments (excluding your mortgage) by your net (take-home) pay. Financial advisers suggest that if this ratio is under 15 percent, you can relax. If it is between 15 and 20 percent, you should be cautious. If it is more than 20 percent, you are dangerously overloaded with debt.

For example, the Walkers have net (take-home) pay of $2,000 per month. Their non-housing debts equal $240 a month. $240 / $2,000 = 12 percent (in the debt "comfort zone")

In contrast, the Tailors have net (take-home) pay of $4,500 and non-housing monthly debts of $990.

$990 / $4,500 = 22 percent (in the debt "danger zone")

Credit card debt. If you have accumulated credit card debt, these debt payments must be included as a budgeted expense. Whereas most consumer debt (such as a car loan) must be paid off in regular monthly installments, most credit cards require only a minimum payment each month. While it may be tempting to budget only this minimum amount, this would be a costly mistake. If you pay only the minimum, it can take years to pay off even a relatively small balance since you primarily are paying the accumulated interest charges rather than the principal.

Because the interest rate on consumer debt is typically high, you should get in the habit of paying down your credit card debt as fast as possible. Make a plan for paying off your existing credit card debt (you may want to consolidate all your credit card debt to the card with the lowest annual percentage rate or APR) and include this as a separate monthly expense. Get in the habit of using only one credit card and pay for all new purchases when you are billed for them each month.

Budget tip: Choose your credit cards wisely. Store-issued credit cards usually carry higher interest rates than bank-issued cards (such as Visa). Compare the annual percentage rate (APR), how the finance charge is calculated, the annual fee (if any), your credit limit, the grace period, and the minimum monthly payment. As a new homeowner you will receive many "pre-approved" credit cards offers. Cut them into small pieces and throw them away.

Cash purchases. It should be easy to track your major fixed expenses and any variable expenses that you pay for by check or credit card. However, your cash purchases also need to be accounted for and allocated to the proper budget category. You may find that you don't have a good handle on your cash purchases—for example, how much you and other family members spend on entertainment, or eating out. In this case, begin with an estimate of your cash expenditures then check your estimate by keeping receipts for all your family's cash expenditures for a two-month period. (If a receipt is not itemized, jot down what it was for.) Then adjust your budget to reflect your actual monthly cash expenditures in various categories.

Budget tip: By making it so easy to withdraw cash, automated teller machines or ATMs may be a budgeter's worst enemy. When you start tracking your cash purchases, you may be surprised at how many of them are impulse purchases. And all those little impulse purchases (a candy bar here, a soda there) can really add up! Also, beware of withdrawal fees charged by banks when you use ATMs. In some instances, you may be charged twice—once by your own bank and once by the bank operating the ATM.

Emergency reserve fund. No homeowner can afford to be without a serious savings plan. You must have a safety net to fall back on should you get sick or laid off from your job. If you don't already have a "nest egg" set aside for emergencies (in a separate money market or other interest-bearing account), you need to begin saving now. Many financial advisers suggest that you "pay yourself first" by saving 5 percent of your take-home pay—$100 per month if your net monthly pay is $2,000. Your goal should be to build up a reserve equal to three to six months worth of expenses. You should never touch this money except in a real emergency. Failure to put aside money for an emergency could mean losing your home in the event of a temporary financial setback. But you have to make this a top priority—if you simply decide to save whatever you have left at the end of each pay period, you're sure to end up with no savings at all.

Step three: Compare your total monthly expenses to your monthly net income...
If your expenses exceed your net income, you are living beyond your means. You can't keep this up for too long before facing a financial crisis. If your net income exceeds your budgeted expenses and you typically run out of money before the end of each pay period, look at your budget closely for expenses you left out. If your net income exceeds your total monthly expenses, skip ahead to step four.

What can you do to cut back on spending and gain solid financial footing? We noted in Chapter 1 that some expenses are "fixed" (such as your mortgage, car payment, and day care) while others are "discretionary"—that is, you have considerable flexibility in deciding how much to spend in these areas (for example, entertainment). If you need to cut back on your spending, you and your family need to look closely at discretionary expenses. It is in these areas where it is easiest to economize. You first need to distinguish between your needs and your wants and then prioritize your wants. This will help you pare down spending, live within your means, and put you on the road to greater financial security.

Budget tip: Although food and clothing are necessities, the amount you spend in these areas is partly discretionary. For example, you might be able to significantly reduce your food budget simply by taking a lunch to school or work. Or you may decide you don't need a new pair of shoes. Or your family might rent a movie a couple of times a month rather than going out to a movie. Carefully evaluate the "extras" that have become ongoing expenses for your family.

Step four: Establish goals…

If your take-home pay exceeds your expenses (and you already have an emergency fund and are paying down your credit card debt), congratulations! It is time for your family to establish some short-term goals (perhaps a home improvement project or a vacation) and long-term goals (such as saving for your children's college education or your own retirement). Think about how much you would need to save each month to achieve one or more goals, and put this money aside in a separate interest-bearing account. For example, if your goal was to purchase new carpeting for the living room in 18 months, and the cost would be approximately $1,350, you would need to save $75 per month.

$1,350 / 18 months = $75 per month

Living Within Your Budget

Creating a budget is a useful exercise in assessing your financial health and in understanding how you spend your money. But a budget is of limited use unless you and your family live by it. Look at your budget each month to monitor your spending and evaluate your progress in meeting your financial goals. If you continue to spend more than you bring in, you need to keep looking for ways to cut back. If you're having trouble following your spending plan, don't give up. Instead, see what other money management plans work for you.

A simple money management tactic that works for some families is the "envelope method." Here's how it works. Let's assume you and your spouse both get paid every other Friday. You make an envelope for each major category of expense and write on it the amount you need to set aside each pay period—for example, mortgage, $525; utilities, $65; day care, $185. For ongoing expenses (such as food and entertainment), write down half the amount budgeted for the month. Now, each payday you cash your paychecks and distribute the cash according to the amounts shown on each envelope. Deposit the cash for your monthly, quarterly, and semi-annual expenses in an interest-bearing checking account.

For discretionary expenditures, you and your family agree to stop spending when the envelope for that spending category is empty. For example, if you spend your entire entertainment allotment in one week, you have to find free leisure activities the following week until the entertainment envelope receives a new allocation from your next paycheck.

Budget tip: Be a wise grocery shopper. Try not to go food shopping when you're hungry. Always shop from a list. Compare unit prices of similar products and of the same product in different size packages. Use coupons. Resist the temptation to use a credit card at the grocery store—pay cash or write a check!

Budget tip: Plan ahead for major purchases rather than making impulsive decisions. Whenever you purchase anything on time, look carefully at the financing terms, including the APR. Often the retailers that offer the easiest terms (no payments due for three months!) actually charge the highest rates. Shop around. Try to save up for things you need rather than charging them. You'll pay less, and you may decide that you'd rather use the money for something else.

Budget tip: Most people find that credit cards create a temptation to spend money they don't have. Get in the habit of using checks or your debit card rather than a credit card to make purchases as well as to pay bills. Close out all credit accounts that you have not used for the last six months.

Getting help. If you're finding it difficult to piece together a workable budget, help is available. Find an NFCC member agency that provides free or low cost, individualized financial counseling and can help you and your family learn to bring your spending under control and get your financial situation in order—before you jeopardize your homeownership.

If the "buy now, pay later" way of life has left you facing a mounting pile of bills each month, you could be headed for real financial trouble. NFCC credit counselors can be reached at (800) 338-2227 or check your local Yellow Pages for other nonprofit credit counseling agencies.

Note: Don't confuse these community-based counseling services with so-called "credit doctors" or "credit repair clinics" that promise to "fix" your bad credit record for a fee. It can't be done.

Reaping the Benefits of Homeownership

Now that you know how to protect your investment by keeping up your house and finances, let's look again at what you have to gain from these increased responsibilities. Of course, the ultimate reward of homeownership is the opportunity to own a debt-free home. When you have paid off the mortgage, you own a valuable asset and, unlike a renter, you no longer have to make monthly payments. But there are other financial benefits of homeownership. At the beginning of Chapter 1, we listed some of these benefits: enforced savings, stable housing costs, increased value, and tax incentives. In the following sections, we explain how tax incentives and use of your equity can benefit you from the start.

Tax Incentives

For many years, the federal government has actively promoted homeownership by providing homeowners with significant tax benefits that are not available to renters. The following is a discussion of some of the homeowner tax benefits. Please consult your tax advisor for more information.

Income tax deductions…
Perhaps in the past you have filed for a tax refund each year using Form 1040-EZ. Now that you are a homeowner and can deduct the interest on your mortgage and other expenses, use Form 1040 (the "long form") and itemize your deductions.

Interest. The deduction for interest alone may save you thousands of dollars in federal income taxes. Especially in the early years, the bulk of your monthly mortgage payment is interest.

For example, suppose you are paying 10 percent interest on an $80,000 fixed-rate mortgage payable over 30 years. Your monthly payments (principal and interest only) are $702, or $8,424 per year. In the first year of the loan, you will pay the lender $7,944 in interest and only $480 in principal!

You can see from Chart 4, "A sample amortization schedule," that each monthly payment is allocated differently between principal and interest. Over time, you pay progressively less interest and more principal. The lender will give you a statement each year showing how much interest you have paid and your year-end principal balance. (You also can ask the lender to provide you with an amortization schedule for your specific loan.)

If you are paying off both a first and second mortgage, the interest you pay on the second is also deductible.

In your first year as a homeowner, your tax break may be even larger since any points you paid to the lender in the process of obtaining your mortgage also count as an interest payment.

Property taxes. Federal law also allows a deduction for taxes on real property paid to state or local jurisdictions. This means that as a homeowner, your real estate (or property) taxes are deductible. Some states allow you to take deductions for these taxes. Low- and moderate-income homeowners also may qualify for a full or partial property tax rebate.

Moving expenses. You may be able to deduct certain moving expenses if the move to your new home was job-related.

Chart 4. A Sample Amortization Schedule

This chart shows a portion of the amortization schedule for a $50,000 mortgage with a 8 percent interest rate repayable over 30 years. The monthly payment is $366.88. It shows how much of each monthly payment goes to repay principal and how much goes toward interest. Note how much more interest a borrower pays in the early years compared to the later years.

Assumptions:

Loan Amount: $50,000.00   Monthly Payment: 366.88

Interest Rate: 8.00%

Term of Loan: 360 Months

Months	Beginning Principal Balance	Interest Paid	Principal Paid	Remaining Principal Balance	Total Interest Paid
1	$ 50,000.00	$ 333.33	$ 33.55	$ 49,966.45	$ 333.33
2	$ 49,966.45	$ 333.11	$ 33.77	$ 49,932.68	$ 666.44
3	$ 49,932.68	$ 332.88	$ 34.00	$ 49,898.68	$ 999.32
4	$ 49,898.68	$ 332.66	$ 34.22	$ 49,864.46	$ 1,331.98
5	$ 49,864.46	$ 332.43	$ 34.45	$ 49,830.01	$ 1,664.41
6	$ 49,830.01	$ 332.20	$ 34.68	$ 49,795.33	$ 1,996.61
7	$ 49,795.33	$ 331.97	$ 34.91	$ 49,760.42	$ 2,328.58
8	$ 49,760.42	$ 331.74	$ 35.14	$ 49,725.28	$ 2,660.32
9	$ 49,725.28	$ 331.50	$ 35.38	$ 49,689.90	$ 2,991.82
10	$ 49,689.90	$ 331.27	$ 35.61	$ 49,654.29	$ 3,323.09
11	$ 49,654.29	$ 331.03	$ 35.85	$ 49,618.44	$ 3,654.12
12	$ 49,618.44	$ 330.79	$ 36.09	$ 49,582.35	$ 3,984.91
13	$ 49,582.35	$ 330.55	$ 36.33	$ 49,546.02	$ 4,315.46
14	$ 49,546.02	$ 330.31	$ 36.57	$ 49,509.45	$ 4,645.77
15	$ 49,509.45	$ 330.06	$ 36.82	$ 49,472.63	$ 4,975.83
16	$ 49,472.63	$ 329.82	$ 37.06	$ 49,435.57	$ 5,305.65
17	$ 49,435.57	$ 329.57	$ 37.31	$ 49,398.26	$ 5,635.22
18	$ 49,398.26	$ 329.32	$ 37.56	$ 49,360.70	$ 5,964.54
19	$ 49,360.70	$ 329.07	$ 37.81	$ 49,322.89	$ 6,293.61
20	$ 49,322.89	$ 328.82	$ 38.06	$ 49,284.83	$ 6,622.43
21	$ 49,284.83	$ 328.57	$ 38.31	$ 49,246.52	$ 6,951.00
22	$ 49,246.52	$ 328.31	$ 38.57	$ 49,207.95	$ 7,279.31
23	$ 49,207.95	$ 328.05	$ 38.83	$ 49,169.12	$ 7,607.36
24	$ 49,169.12	$ 327.79	$ 39.09	$ 49,130.03	$ 7,935.15

Payments #25 through #330 are not reprinted here

Continued

Chart 4. A Sample Amortization Schedule, Cont.

Months	Beginning Principal Balance	Interest Paid	Principal Paid	Remaining Principal Balance	Total Interest Paid
337	$ 8,114.58	$ 54.10	$ 312.78	$ 7,801.80	$ 81,440.36
338	$ 7,801.80	$ 52.01	$ 314.87	$ 7,486.93	$ 81,492.37
339	$ 7,486.93	$ 49.91	$ 316.97	$ 7,169.96	$ 81,542.28
340	$ 7,169.96	$ 47.80	$ 319.08	$ 6,850.88	$ 81,590.08
341	$ 6,850.88	$ 45.67	$ 321.21	$ 6,529.67	$ 81,635.75
342	$ 6,529.67	$ 43.53	$ 323.35	$ 6,206.32	$ 81,679.28
343	$ 6,206.32	$ 41.38	$ 325.50	$ 5,880.82	$ 81,720.66
344	$ 5,880.82	$ 39.21	$ 327.67	$ 5,553.15	$ 81,759.87
345	$ 5,553.15	$ 37.02	$ 329.86	$ 5,223.29	$ 81,796.89
346	$ 5,223.29	$ 34.82	$ 332.06	$ 4,891.23	$ 81,831.71
347	$ 4,891.23	$ 32.61	$ 334.27	$ 4,556.96	$ 81,864.32
348	$ 4,556.96	$ 30.38	$ 336.50	$ 4,220.46	$ 81,894.70
349	$ 4,220.46	$ 28.14	$ 338.74	$ 3,881.72	$ 81,922.84
350	$ 3,881.72	$ 25.88	$ 341.00	$ 3,540.72	$ 81,948.72
351	$ 3,540.72	$ 23.60	$ 343.28	$ 3,197.44	$ 81,972.32
352	$ 3,197.44	$ 21.32	$ 345.56	$ 2,851.88	$ 81,993.64
353	$ 2,851.88	$ 19.01	$ 347.87	$ 2,504.01	$ 82,012.65
354	$ 2,504.01	$ 16.69	$ 350.19	$ 2,153.82	$ 82,029.34
355	$ 2,153.82	$ 14.36	$ 352.52	$ 1,801.30	$ 82,043.70
356	$ 1,801.30	$ 12.01	$ 354.87	$ 1,446.43	$ 82,055.71
357	$ 1,446.43	$ 9.64	$ 357.24	$ 1,089.19	$ 82,065.35
358	$ 1,089.19	$ 7.26	$ 359.62	$ 729.57	$ 82,072.61
359	$ 729.57	$ 4.86	$ 362.02	$ 367.55	$ 82,077.47
360	$ 367.55	$ 2.45	$ 367.55	$ 0.00	$ 82,079.92

★ Chart shows principal and interest only. These are approximations for demonstration purposes only. Does not represent any warranty, express or implied, of applicability to a particular financial transaction.

Rental property. If part of your home is rented out (for example, your basement has been converted into a "garden apartment"), the rent you receive must be reported for income tax purposes. However, you can deduct from the rent repair costs and operating expenses, such as utilities, insurance, and advertising for tenants, as well as an annual depreciation allowance. If your deductions are greater than your rental income, you can report a loss (subject to limitations), which will lower your taxable income.

Keeping records. For tax purposes it's important to keep accurate and complete records of the cost of any improvements. Although the cost of improvements is not deductible, they increase your home's "basis"—which in turn determines the amount of your gain for tax purposes when you sell it. (Some of the closing costs when you bought your house also can increase the home's "basis" when you sell. So keep your settlement sheet in a safe place with your other important papers!)

Using your Homeowner's Equity

Another financial advantage of homeownership is that as you pay down your mortgage over time, you build up equity. This means that even though you don't own your home outright, your investment has a cash value. Your equity also increases if the market value of your house increases. Stated as a formula, your equity equals the current market value of your property minus the amount you still owe on the mortgage. If your house currently is valued at $120,000 and you owe the lender $85,000, you have $35,000 equity in the house. This may be considerably more than you paid toward the purchase of the property.

Let's look now at some of the ways you can "use" your equity without selling the house.

Second mortgage...
One way to take advantage of the equity in your home is to take out a second mortgage. This is a loan for a specified amount for a specific purpose (for example, a major home improvement project) and is repayable over a fixed period. It differs from a personal loan in that your property serves as security for the loan. The interest rate on such a loan typically will be higher than the interest rate on a first mortgage but less than an unsecured loan.

Home equity line of credit...
Another way to take advantage of the equity you have invested in your home is to take out a home equity line of credit. This type of loan enables homeowners to qualify for a sizable amount of credit at a low interest rate (typically a variable rather than fixed rate). Because the debt is secured by your home, all or part of the interest is deductible regardless of what you use your credit line for. (See a tax advisor or call the IRS for details on the deductibility of interest on a home equity line.)

A line of credit is a form of revolving credit, which means that as you repay what you have borrowed, your line of credit is restored in that amount. Most home equity plans allow you to borrow up to your credit limit for a set time period, such as 10 years. However, you pay interest only on what you borrow. When the plan expires, the entire outstanding balance typically comes due. Be sure you understand the terms of the loan because failure to repay the loan at the end of the term could result in the loss of your home.

Beware of Predatory Lenders...
Although most lenders are trustworthy, unfortunately some are not. Home equity loans can be an opportunity for predatory lenders to take advantage of you. Watch out for the following practices to avoid a situation that may cost you your home:

- Unusually high interest rates;
- Excessive points or origination fees;
- Padded closing costs;
- High broker fees;
- Unnecessary costs such as pre-paid credit life insurance;
- High pressure or door-to-door sales;
- Excessive pre-payment penalties;
- Encouragement to borrow more than you need or more than the value of your home;
- A loan based on equity in the home, not your ability to repay the loan; and
- Improper disclosure or terms that change at the last minute.

To get the best loan available to you while avoiding predatory lenders, compare up-front costs, terms, and interest rates with several lenders. Be sure to read all loan documents carefully, and understand all of the terms completely. Don't be pressured into a loan for any reason, including a situation that involves borrowing more than you need and can afford to repay. If you're unsure about whether you are making the right decision, check with a nonprofit housing or credit counseling agency.

Your home as a saleable asset...
Of course, you can always turn your home into cash by selling it. The fact that many homeowners don't stay in the first home they buy makes it prudent to consider the resale value of a home from the outset, especially if you plan to undertake costly renovations.

Refinancing Your Home

If interest rates are falling, you may be able to significantly reduce your monthly mortgage payment by refinancing. Refinancing involves taking out a new mortgage at a lower interest rate and using it to pay off your existing mortgage. Even if your new loan is with the same lender, refinancing involves going through closing (including payment of closing costs) all over again. Because of this, the standard "rule of thumb" is to refinance only if interest rates have dropped at least two percentage points below the rate you are paying and you plan to stay put for at least a couple of years. A prepayment penalty on your present mortgage could be the greatest deterrent to refinancing. Be sure to double check your mortgage documents before you proceed with a refinance.

Prepaying Your Mortgage

At some point your monthly payment may seem much more manageable than it does today. As your income rises, your mortgage payment will be a smaller percentage of your total income. At that time, you may want to pay off your mortgage faster—especially if you realize how much interest you are paying.

You can easily save substantial amounts in interest payments over the life of your mortgage by making extra payments, either on a regular basis or even occasionally. Most lenders have a place on the payment coupon marked "additional principal payments" just for this purpose. If you were to make one extra payment per year (for example, when you receive an income tax refund), you would pay off your mortgage years ahead of schedule. Even paying a small amount extra each month will save you in interest since the entire amount goes to pay down the principal. If you paid $50 extra each month on a 30-year mortgage with a beginning principal balance of $80,000, borrowed at a fixed rate of 8 percent, you would pay off your loan over seven years early, and you would save over $37,000 in interest.

Summary

Although buying a home takes time and hard work, it is perhaps the greatest financial investment you will ever make. It is essential that you protect this investment by following a regular home maintenance program and developing a sound financial management plan. If you ever find that you are unable to keep up with your monthly payments, be sure to contact the lender immediately to discuss the situation and work out a solution. If you cooperate with the lender, you may be able to avoid foreclosure and the loss of your home. As you pay down your mortgage over time and the market value of your home increases, you will have the satisfaction of knowing that you are building up substantial equity for the future. Good luck, and we hope you will enjoy the many benefits of homeownership!

Glossary

Acceleration clause. A provision in a mortgage that allows the lender to demand payment of the entire outstanding balance if a monthly payment is missed.

Adjustable-rate mortgage (ARM). A mortgage that permits the lender to adjust its interest rate periodically when a specified index changes.

Amortization. The gradual repayment of a mortgage by installments, calculated to pay off the obligation at the end of a fixed period of time.

Amortization schedule. A timetable for payment of a mortgage showing the amount of each payment applied to interest and principal and the balance remaining.

Annual percentage rate (APR). The total cost of a mortgage stated as a yearly rate; includes such items as the base interest rate, loan origination fee (points), commitment fees, prepaid interest, and other credit costs, which may be paid by the borrower.

Appraisal. A professional opinion or estimate of the market value of a property.

Appreciation. An increase in the value of a property due to changes in market conditions or other causes.

Assessed value. The valuation placed on property by a public tax assessor that is used to compute property taxes.

Assumable mortgage. A mortgage that can be taken over ("assumed") by the buyer when a home is sold.

Assumption. The transfer of the seller's existing mortgage to the buyer.

Binder. A preliminary agreement between a buyer and seller, which includes the price and terms of the contract.

Cap. A provision of an ARM limiting how much the interest rate or mortgage payments may increase or decrease.

Cash reserve. A requirement of some lenders that buyers after closing have two months' mortgage payments in cash.

Clear title. A title free of liens or legal questions as to ownership of property.

Closing. A meeting at which a sale of a property is finalized by delivery of a deed from seller to buyer and the buyer signing the mortgage documents and paying closing costs. Also called "settlement."

Closing costs. Expenses (over and above the price of the property) incurred by buyers and sellers in transferring ownership of a property. Also called "settlement costs."

Commitment letter. A formal offer by a lender stating the terms under which it agrees to lend money to a homebuyer.

Condominium. A form of property ownership in which the homeowner holds title to an individual dwelling unit, an undivided interest in common areas of a multi-unit project, and sometimes the exclusive use of certain limited common areas.

Contingency. A condition that must be met before a contract is legally binding.

Conventional mortgage. Any mortgage that is not insured or guaranteed by the federal government.

Convertible ARM. An adjustable-rate mortgage that can be converted to a fixed-rate mortgage under specified conditions.

Cooperative. A type of multiple ownership in which the residents of a multi-unit housing complex own shares in the corporation that owns the property, giving each resident the right to occupy a specific apartment or unit.

Covenant. A clause in a mortgage that obligates or restricts the borrower and which, if violated, can result in foreclosure.

Credit report. A report of an individual's credit history prepared by a credit bureau or consumer reporting agency and used by a lender in determining a loan applicant's credit-worthiness.

Credit Score. A score-based statistical method used to predict the likelihood that you will repay a credit obligation, such as a mortgage loan. The most well-known credit score in the mortgage industry has been developed by Fair Isaac Corporation and often is referred to as a FICO score.

Deed. The legal document conveying title to a property.

Deed of trust. The document used in some states instead of a mortgage, which gives the lender a security interest in the property. Title is conveyed to a trustee by the borrower (who retains equitable title). When the debt is paid in full, title is reconveyed to the borrower.

Default. The failure to make a mortgage payment on a timely basis or otherwise comply with other requirements of a mortgage.

Delinquency. A loan in which a payment is overdue but not yet in default.

Deposit. See earnest money.

Depreciation. A decline in the value of property; the opposite of "appreciation."

Discount points. See points.

Down payment. The part of the purchase price, which the buyer pays in cash and does not finance with a mortgage.

Due-on-sale clause. A provision in a mortgage allowing the lender to demand repayment in full if the borrower sells the property securing the mortgage.

Earnest money. A deposit made by the potential homebuyer to show that he or she is serious about buying the house.

Easement. A right of way giving persons other than the owner access to, or over, a property.

Equal Credit Opportunity Act (ECOA). A federal law that prohibits lenders from discriminating on the basis of the borrower's race, color, religion, national origin, age, sex, marital status, or receipt of income from public assistance programs.

Equity. A homeowner's financial interest in a property. Equity is the difference between the fair market value of a property and the amount still owed on the mortgage.

Equity loan. A loan based on the borrower's equity in his or her home.

Escrow. The holding of documents and money by a neutral third party prior to closing; also, an account held by the lender (or servicer) into which a homeowner pays money for taxes and insurance.

Fair Credit Reporting Act. A consumer protection law that regulates the disclosure of consumer credit reports by consumer credit reporting agencies and establishes procedures for correcting mistakes on a credit record.

Fannie Mae and Freddie Mac. Both organizations were chartered by Congress to increase the supply of funds that mortgage lenders, such as commercial banks, mortgage bankers, savings institutions and credit unions, can make available to homebuyers. Fannie Mae and Freddie Mac buy mortgages from lenders, packaging the mortgages into securities and selling them to investors. Fannie Mae and Freddie Mac only buy loans that meet their guidelines and play an important role in setting criteria used to evaluate a mortgage application.

FHA mortgage. A mortgage that is insured by the Federal Housing Administration. Also referred to as a "government" mortgage.

FHA 203(k) Rehabilitation Mortgages. FHA-insured Section 203(k) rehabilitation first mortgages enable borrowers to purchase and rehabilitate homes. With this mortgage product, borrowers can qualify for loan amounts based on the "as-completed" value of the property, up to the maximum FHA loan limits.

FHA Title I Home Improvement Loans. Title I home improvement loans may be used to finance modest home improvements when homeowners have little equity in their property. Title I loans generally are based on the creditworthiness of the borrower, rather than the equity in the home.

FICO Score. See credit score.

First mortgage. A mortgage that has first claim to the secured property in the event of default.

Fixed-rate mortgage. A mortgage in which the interest rate does not change during the entire term of the loan.

Flood insurance. Insurance that compensates for physical property damages resulting from flooding. It is required for properties located in federally designated flood areas.

Forbearance. The lender's postponement of foreclosure to give the borrower time to catch up on overdue payments.

Foreclosure. The legal process by which a mortgaged property may be sold when a mortgage is in default.

Graduated payment mortgage. A mortgage that starts with low monthly payments that increase at a predetermined rate for a specified time. The initial monthly payments are set at an amount lower than those required for full debt amortization.

Hazard insurance. Insurance coverage that compensates for physical damage to a property from fire, wind, vandalism, or other hazards.

Homeowner's insurance. An insurance policy that combines personal liability coverage and hazard insurance coverage for a dwelling and its contents.

Homeowner's warranty. A type of insurance that covers repairs to specified parts of a house for a specific period of time. It is provided by the builder or property seller as a condition of the sale.

HUD-1. See settlement sheet.

Interest. The fee charged for borrowing money.

Interest rate cap. A provision of an ARM limiting how much interest rates may increase per adjustment period or over the life of a mortgage. See also lifetime cap.

Joint tenancy. A form of co-ownership giving each tenant equal interest and equal rights in the property, including the right of survivorship.

Late charge. The penalty a borrower must pay when a payment is made after the due date.

Lease-purchase mortgage loan. A mortgage product that allows low- and moderate-income homebuyers to lease a home from a nonprofit organization with an option to buy. Each month's rent payment consists of PITI payments on the first mortgage, plus an extra amount earmarked for deposit to a savings account where down payment accumulates.

Lien. A legal claim against a property that must be paid off when the property is sold.

Lifetime cap. A provision of an ARM that limits the total increase in interest rates over the life of the loan.

Loan commitment. See commitment letter.

Loan servicing. The collection of mortgage payments from borrowers and related responsibilities of a loan servicer.

Loan-to-value percentage (LTV). The relationship between the unpaid principal balance of the mortgage and the appraised value (or sales price if it is lower) of the property.

Lock-in. A written agreement guaranteeing the homebuyer a specified interest rate provided the loan is closed within a set period of time. The lock-in usually specifies the number of points to be paid at closing.

Mortgage. A legal document that pledges a property to the lender as security for payment of a debt.

Mortgage banker. A company that originates mortgages exclusively for resale in the secondary market.

Mortgage broker. An individual or company that for a fee acts as intermediary between borrowers and lenders.

Mortgage insurance. See private mortgage insurance.

Mortgage insurance premium (MIP). The fee paid by a borrower to FHA or a private insurer for mortgage insurance.

Mortgage margin. The set percentage the lender adds to the index value to determine the interest rate of an ARM.

Mortgage note. A legal document obligating a borrower to repay a loan at a stated interest rate during a specified period of time; the mortgage note is secured by a mortgage.

Mortgage interest rate. The rate of interest in effect for the monthly payment due.

Mortgagee. The lender in a mortgage agreement.

Mortgagor. The borrower in a mortgage agreement.

Negative amortization. A gradual increase in the mortgage debt that occurs when the monthly payment is not large enough to cover the entire amount of principal and interest due. The amount of the shortfall is added to the unpaid principal balance, which results in "negative" amortization.

Notice of default. A formal written notice to a borrower that a default has occurred and that legal action may be taken.

Origination fee. A fee paid to a lender for processing a loan application; it is stated as a percentage of the mortgage amount.

Owner financing. A property purchase transaction in which the seller provides all or part of the financing.

Payment cap. A provision of some ARMs limiting the amount a borrower's payments may increase regardless of any interest rate increase, may result in negative amortization. See adjustable-rate mortgage.

PITI. Stands for principal, interest, taxes, and insurance—the components of a monthly mortgage payment.

Planned unit developments (PUDs). A planned unit development is a project or subdivision that consists of common property that is owned and maintained by an owners' association for the individual PUD unit owners.

Points. A one-time charge by the lender to increase the yield of the loan; a point is 1 percent of the mortgage amount.

Prepaids. Fees collected at closing to cover items such as setting up escrow accounts for property taxes, homeowner's insurance, and private mortgage insurance premiums.

Prepayment penalty. A fee that may be charged to a borrower who pays off a loan before it is due.

Prequalification. The process of determining how much money a prospective homebuyer will be eligible to borrow before applying for a loan.

Principal. The amount borrowed or remaining unpaid; also, that part of the monthly payment that reduces the outstanding balance of a mortgage.

Private mortgage insurance (PMI). Non-government-provided insurance, which protects lenders against loss if a borrower defaults. Fannie Mae generally requires private mortgage insurance for loans with loan-to-value (LTV) percentages greater than 80 percent.

Purchase and sale agreement. A written contract signed by the buyer and seller stating the terms and conditions under which a property will be sold.

Qualifying ratios. Guidelines applied by the lenders to determine how large a loan to grant a homebuyer.

Radon. An invisible, odorless gas found in some homes; may cause health problems in sufficient concentrations.

Rate lock. See lock-in.

Real estate sales professional. A person licensed to negotiate and transact the sale of real estate on behalf of the property owner.

Real Estate Settlement Procedures Act. A consumer protection law that, among other things, requires lenders to give borrowers advance notice of closing costs.

Refinancing. The process of paying off one loan with the proceeds from a new loan using the same property as security.

Rent with option to buy. See lease-purchase mortgage loan.

Second mortgage. A mortgage that has a lien position subordinate to the first mortgage.

Secondary mortgage market. The buying and selling of existing mortgages. See Fannie Mae and Freddie Mac.

Seller-take-back. An agreement in which the owner of a property provides financing, often in combination with an assumed mortgage.

Settlement. See closing.

Settlement sheet. The computation of costs payable at closing that determines the seller's net proceeds and the buyer's net payment (referred to as a HUD-1).

Survey. A drawing or map showing the precise legal boundaries of a property, the location of improvements, easements, rights of way, encroachments, and other physical features.

Tenancy by entirety. A type of joint ownership of property that provides rights of survivorship and is available only to a husband and wife.

Tenancy in common. A type of joint ownership in a property without rights of survivorship.

Title. A legal document evidencing a person's right to or ownership of a property.

Title company. A company that specializes in examining and insuring titles to real estate.

Title insurance. Insurance to protect the lender (lender's policy) or the buyer (owner's policy) against loss from disputes over ownership of property.

Title search. An examination of the public records to ensure that the seller is the legal owner of the property and that there are no liens or other claims outstanding.

Transfer tax. State or local tax payable when title passes from one owner to another.

Truth-in-Lending Act. A federal law that requires lenders to disclose in writing the terms and conditions of a mortgage, including the APR and other charges.

Underwriting. The process of evaluating a loan application to determine the risk involved for the lender. It involves an analysis of the borrower's creditworthiness and the quality of the property itself.

WORKSHEET 1
Your Current Monthly Expenses

Use this worksheet to calculate your current monthly expenses. By comparing your non-housing expenses to your gross monthly income (in Worksheet 3), you can see how much you have left for housing-related expenses. As a homeowner, your housing expenses will include your monthly mortgage payment, property taxes and homeowner's insurance, condominium fee (if applicable), utilities, and maintenance costs.

	Average Monthly Payment
Current Housing Expenses	
Rent	$
Utilities (if paid separately)	$
Current Non-Housing Expenses	
Food	$
Clothing	$
Day care/tuition	$
Car loan	$
Car insurance	$
Gas and oil	$
Car repairs	$
Health care	$
Credit card payments	$
Installment loan payments	$
Student loan	$
Alimony/child support	$
Entertainment	$
Taxes	$
Telephone	$
Insurance (other than car)	$
Other (specify)	$
Other (specify)	$
Savings	$
Total Monthly Expenses and Savings	$

WORKSHEET 2
Your Available Cash and Assets

List here all your sources of cash and any assets you can use for the down payment and closing costs.

Checking account(s)	$
Savings account(s)	$
Mutual funds, stocks, and bonds	$
Cash value of life insurance policy	$
Cash gifts from parents or other relatives	$
Other assets	$
Total cash and assets	$

WORKSHEET 3
Your Gross Monthly Income

List all current, regular gross monthly income for yourself and any co-borrowers. Consider all sources of income during the past 12 months, if they are likely to continue for at least three years.

	Average Monthly Amount
Gross pay (before taxes and other deductions)	$
Overtime/part-time/seasonal/commissions	$
Bonuses/tips	$
Dividends/interest earnings	$
Business or investment earnings	$
Pension/Social Security benefits	$
Veterans Administration benefits	$
Unemployment compensation	$
Public assistance	$
Alimony, child support, or separate maintenance income	$
Other	$
Total gross monthly income	$

WORKSHEET 4
Your Monthly Debt Payments

List all the monthly debt obligations of your household (other than your current housing expenses).

If your total monthly debt payments equal more than 8 percent—or 10 percent if you have very good credit—of your gross monthly income (which you calculated on Worksheet 3), then your "excess debt" will reduce the amount of mortgage for which you can qualify.

Refer to Chart 3 for additional detail.

	Average Monthly Amount
Car payment	$
Other installment loan payments with 10 or more monthly payments remaining (for example, furniture, appliance, etc.)	$
Average monthly credit card payment	$
Student loan payment	$
Medical/health care payment	$
Alimony/child support payment	$
Total monthly debt payments	$

WORKSHEET 5
Calculating Your Maximum Mortgage

To compute your maximum mortgage amount for a loan, you must use the lender's qualifying guidelines. Typically you must find the lower of two numbers—(1) the Housing Expense Ratio (typically 28 percent) and the (2) Total Debt Ratio (typically 36 percent). Special loans like those the affordable loan products from Fannie Mae and Freddie Mac allow these numbers to be higher, which will allow you to qualify for a larger loan.

Housing Expense Ratio (1)

Total gross monthly income (from Worksheet 3)	$_____	
Multiplied by 28 percent	$_____ x .28	
Maximum allowable for PITI plus homeowners' association or condo fee	$_____ (1)	

Total Debt Ratio (2)

Total gross monthly income (from Worksheet 3)	$_____	
x 36 percent =	$_____ x .36	
Maximum allowable for PITI plus homeowners' association or condo fee and other monthly debts	$_____	
Minus Total Monthly Debt Payments (from Worksheet 4)	- _____	
Maximum allowable for PITI plus homeowners' association or condo fee	$_____ (2)	
Choose the lower of (1) or (2)	$_____ (3)	

THIS FIGURE REPRESENTS THE MAXIMUM ALLOWABLE FOR PITI, GIVEN YOUR CURRENT GROSS MONTHLY INCOME AND DEBTS.

Multiply (3) by 80 percent★ to estimate portion of PITI that represents P&I only	$_____ (3)
x .80	
MAXIMUM ALLOWABLE FOR P&I	$_____ (4)

WORKSHEET 5
Continued

Divide the MAXIMUM ALLOWABLE FOR P&I by the factor in the chart below closest to today's interest rates.

Interest rate	30–year P&I Factor
5.5%	.00568
6.0%	.00600
6.5%	.00632
7.0%	.00665
7.5%	.00699
8.0%	.00734
8.5%	.00769
9.0%	.00805
9.5%	.00841
10.0%	.00878
10.5%	.00915
11.0%	.00953

$ _____ divided by _____ = $ _____ = MAXIMUM LOAN (P&I)
(P&I FACTOR)   AMOUNT
(4) above

WORKSHEET 6
Your Housing Priorities

This questionnaire (prepared with assistance from the National Association of Realtors®) should help you assess your house-hunting requirements. Circle your choices (especially when presented with an "OR") and fill in the blanks. Try to be as realistic and practical as possible!

Type of home	Existing OR newly built
	One level OR multi-story
	Traditional OR contemporary
Construction	Brick OR wood siding OR cement OR cedar shingles OR other
Lot	Size
Rooms—type and number	Bedroom(s): #
	Bath(s): #
	Dining
	Kitchen (space for eat-in table/chairs OR no)
	Family
	Laundry room
	Basement
	Attic space
	Storage requirements
	Other
Floors and covering	Hardwood OR wall-to-wall carpeting OR mix
Extras	Fireplace (gas OR wood-burning)
	Garage: # of cars:
	Porch OR deck OR patio
	Pool Irrigation OR sprinkler system
	Security system
	Air-conditioning (central OR window)
Heat	Forced air OR radiator OR other
Fuel	Gas OR oil OR passive solar OR other
Overall energy efficiency	Could qualify for an energy efficiency mortgage or local Energy Star savings program
Transportation requirements	
School requirements	
Access to grocery and other shopping	
Church requirements	
Price range	$ to $
Cash down payment available	$
Special requirements or preferences	

WORKSHEET 7
Housing Evaluation Checklist

Address:

The MLS printout provided by the real estate sales agent should provide the following:

Asking price:

Annual property taxes:

Average monthly utility costs:

What is the seller's current mortgage balance and monthly payments?

Is the seller willing to take back a second mortgage?

Is the seller's current mortgage assumable? If so, what is the interest rate?

Neighborhood	Ideal	Acceptable	Poor
Are many houses for sale in the area? If so, why?			
Are there plans underway to change the zoning regulations? If so, how will that affect the neighborhood?			
Is it convenient to public transportation?			
To shopping?			
Recreational facilities?			
Schools?			
Churches?			

Whether the house is new or old, both the quality of the building materials and the craftsmanship as well as the condition are important considerations.

Type of home and construction

How well insulated is the house?

Are the windows energy efficient?

Is the roof in good condition?

Does the house appear to have been well maintained?

Floor plan: good traffic flow from one room to another?

Bedroom(s)   Number: _____
                                                  On which floor(s)? _____

Gas OR oil OR passive solar OR other

Bathroom(s)   Number: _____ (full)
                                                  _____ (half)
                                                  On which floor(s)? _____

Dining room

Kitchen (space for eat-in table/chairs?) Any built-in appliances?

Family room

Laundry room

Basement

   Is the basement finished? Does it flood after every heavy rain?

Attic space

Storage

Floors and covering

Heat

Fuel

Extras

Fireplace (gas OR wood-burning)

Garage: # of cars:

Porch OR deck OR patio

Pool

Irrigation OR Sprinkler system

Air-conditioning (central OR room)

Security system

Remarks

WORKSHEET 8
Lender Mortgage Rates/Fees Checklist

Make copies of this checklist and use it to compare mortgage rates and fees when you contact lenders.

	#1	#2
Name of lender		
Name of contact		
Phone number		
Web site address		
Amount of mortgage you need		
Types of mortgage available (fixed-rate, ARM, FHA, VA, etc.)		
Interest rate		
Points		
APR		
Loan term (15, 20, 30 years)		
Fees:		
• Application	$	$
• Origination	$	$
• Credit report	$	$
• Document preparation	$	$
• Under writing	$	$
• Appraisal	$	$
• Survey (is one required?)	$	$
• Courier	$	$
• Flood certification	$	$
• Tax service	$	$
• Assumption (if applicable)	$	$
• Fees for lender's attorney	$	$
• Title search and insurance	$	$
• Other	$	$
• Other	$	$
Average time required to process and under write mortgage		
Application options:		
• Face-to-face meeting		
• Via telephone and FAX machine		
• Online application		
Minimum down payment required:		
• Without PMI	%	%
• With PMI		

WORKSHEET 8
Continued

If PMI is required:		
• Up-front cost	$	$
• Monthly premiums	$	$
• When may it be cancelled?		
Name of lender #1		#2
• Lock-in:		
• Upon approval OR at application?		
• Interest rate AND points locked-in?		
• Written agreement?		
• Lasts how long?		
Prepayment:		
• Is there a penalty?		
• Are extra payments allowed?		
Assumable?		
Escrow required for taxes and insurance?		
Available payment options:		
• Monthly only		
• Biweekly		
• Automatic deduction		
ARMs only:		
• Initial interest rate		
• Adjusted how frequently?		
• Index		
• Margin		
Rate caps:		
• Periodic		
• Lifetime		
Payment cap:		
• Can negative amortization occur?		
• If so, is maximum LTV (including negative amortization) capped?		
If convertible:		
• When can you convert to a fixed-rate mortgage?		
• Fees		
• Index used		
• Margin used		
Comments		

WORKSHEET 9
Pre-Application Worksheet

Borrower's name _____

Social Security # _____

Current address _____

Home phone number: (   )_____   Work phone number: (   )_____

Co-borrower's name _____

Borrower's name _____

Social Security # _____

Current address _____

Home phone number: (   )_____   Work phone number: (   )_____

Co-borrower's name _____

Borrower's name _____

Social Security # _____

Current address _____

Home phone number: (   )_____   Work phone number: (   )_____

Co-borrower's name _____

Borrower's name _____

Social Security # _____

Current address _____

Home phone number: (   )_____   Work phone number: (   )_____

Address of house you are buying _____

Price of house $ _____

Mortgage amount you are applying for $ _____

Type of loan _____

Term (15, 20, 30 years) _____

WORKSHEET 9
Continued

Each borrower who is applying for the mortgage loan should fill out the following:

Employment (past two years) — Start with current employment first

Name of Employer	Address of Employer	Dates you worked there	Current or ending salary

Bank Accounts — Checking, Savings, etc.

Name of Bank	Address of Bank	Account Number	Type of Account	Estimated Current Balance

Landlords (Past Two Years)

Name of Landlord	Address	Dates You Rented

Credit Cards — Department Stores, Banks, etc.

Name of Creditor	Address	Account Number	Monthly Payment You Make	Estimated Balance You Owe

Loan Information — Car, Student, etc.

Name of Creditor	Address	Account Number	Monthly Payment You Make	Estimated Balance You Owe

Previous Credit References — Paid-off loans and other credit

Name of Lender	Account Address	Type of Number	Date You Loan	Paid It Off

Remember to bring the following with you:

✓ Personal check for loan application fee

✓ Purchase and sale agreement

✓ Copy of real estate listing of house you are buying

✓ Photocopy of earnest money check

Each borrower on the loan application should bring:

✓ Payroll stub(s) from employer, W-2 forms for past two years, or other proof of employment and salary (if self-employed: balance sheets, tax returns for the past two years, and year-to-date profit and loss statement)

✓ Photocopies of last three monthly bank statements for all checking and savings accounts

✓ Company name, number, and value of stocks and bonds you own

✓ Make, year, and value of all automobiles you own

✓ Information on real estate you already own

✓ If establishing a nontraditional credit history: canceled checks or money order receipts as evidence of rental, utility, or other payments

WORKSHEET 10
Settlement Costs Worksheet

Use this form to compare costs when shopping for a settlement agent to handle your closing.

Title Charges:	Paid from borrower's funds at settlement	Paid from seller's funds at settlement
Settlement or closing fee	$	$
Abstract or title search	$	$
Title examination	$	$
Title insurance binder	$	$
Document preparation fee	$	$
Notary fees	$	$
Attorney's fees	$	$
Title insurance:		
Lender's coverage	$	$
Owner's coverage	$	$

WORKSHEET 11
Seasonal Maintenance Checklist

Fall Checklist

Outside

✓ Check all weather stripping and caulking around windows and doors. Replace or repair as needed.

✓ Check for cracks and holes in house siding; fill with caulking as necessary.

✓ Remove window air conditioner, or put weatherproof covers on them.

✓ Take down screens (if removable type); clean and store them.

✓ Drain outside faucets.

✓ Clean gutters and drain pipes so they won't be clogged with leaves.

✓ Check roof for leaks; repair as necessary.

✓ Check flashing around vents, skylights, and chimneys for leaks.

✓ Check chimney for damaged chimney caps and loose or missing mortar.

✓ Check chimney flue; clean obstructions and make sure damper closes tightly.

✓ Clean siding. Paint or seal if you have wood siding.

✓ Inspect wood framing for termites; re-treat as necessary.

Inside

✓ Check insulation wherever possible; replace or add as necessary.

✓ Have heating system and heat pump serviced; have humidifier checked; change or clean filters on furnace.

✓ Drain hot water heater and remove sediment from bottom of tank; clean burner surfaces; adjust burners.

✓ Check all faucets for leaks; replace washers if necessary.

✓ Check and clean humidifier in accordance with manufacturer's instructions.

✓ Clean refrigerator coils.

✓ Test and check batteries on smoke and carbon monoxide detectors.

Spring Checklist

Outside

✓ Check all weather stripping and caulking around windows and doors, especially if you have air-conditioning.

✓ Check house for cracked or peeled paint; caulk and repaint as necessary.

✓ Remove, clean, and store storm windows (if removable).

✓ Check all door and window screens; patch or replace as needed; put screens up (if removable type).

✓ Check for cracks or surface deterioration if you have a concrete or block foundation. Consult a professional if you have any leaking or severe cracking.

✓ Inspect roof for missing or deteriorated shingles.

✓ Clean exterior and garage doors; refinish when necessary.

WORKSHEET 11
Continued

Inside

✓ Replace filters on air conditioners.

✓ Check and clean dryer vent, stove hood, and room fans; change or clean filters on furnace.

✓ Check seals on refrigerator and freezer; clean refrigerator coils.

✓ Clean fireplace; leave damper open for improved ventilation if home is not air conditioned.

✓ Check basement wall and floors for dampness; if too moist, remedy as appropriate.

✓ Clean dehumidifier according to manufacturer's instructions.

✓ Check for leaky faucets; replace washers as necessary.

✓ Check attic for proper ventilation; open vents.

✓ Clean drapes and blinds; repair as needed.

✓ Test and check batteries on smoke and carbon monoxide detectors.

WORKSHEET 12
Your Monthly Budget

Net Monthly Income

Total Gross Monthly Income (from Worksheet 3★)		$ _____
minus Payroll Deductions	−	$ _____
Total Net Monthly Income		$ _____

Monthly Expenses/Savings

Current Housing Expenses		$ _____
Monthly Mortgage Payment		$ _____
Property Taxes and Insurance (if not included in mortgage payment)	+	$ _____
Average Monthly Utilities	+	$ _____
Allowance for Maintenance Expenses	+	$ _____
Non-Housing Expenses (from Worksheet 4#)	+	$ _____
Savings (Emergency Fund)	+	$ _____
Total Monthly Expenses and Savings		$ _____

Remaining Discretionary Income

Total Net Income		$ _____
minus Total Monthly Expenses/Savings	+	$ _____
Funds Available for Short- and Long-Term Investments		$ _____

Investment Goals	*Total Amount Needed*	*Monthly Savings*
1.	$ _____	$ _____
2.	$ _____	$ _____
3.	$ _____	$ _____
Long-Term Goals		
1.	$ _____	$ _____
2.	$ _____	$ _____
3.	$ _____	$ _____

★Note: Don't include from Worksheet 3 any income that won't come in each month—for example, bonuses or occasional seasonal employment.

#Note: Don't include any expenses deducted from your paycheck. Include the debt payments you listed in Worksheet 4.

Notes

Notes

Notes

Notes